U.S. Department of Justice
Office of Justice Programs
Bureau of Justice Statistics

December 2013, NCJ 243920

Prisoners in 2012

Trends in Admissions and Releases, 1991–2012

Bulletin

E. Ann Carson and Daniela Golinelli, *BJS Statisticians*

The prisoner population in the United States in 2012 declined for the third straight year, from 1,599,000 at yearend 2011 to 1,570,400 at yearend 2012. On December 31, 2012, the number of persons sentenced to serve more than 1 year (1,511,500) in state or federal prison facilities decreased by 27,400 prisoners from yearend 2011 and by 42,600 from yearend 2009, when the U.S. prison population was at its peak (figure 1). Between 1978 and 2009, the number of prisoners held in federal and state facilities in the United States increased almost 430%, from 294,400 on December 31, 1978, to 1,555,600 on December 31, 2009. This growth occurred because the number of prison admissions exceeded the number of releases from state prisons each year. However, in 2009, prison releases exceeded admissions for the first time in more than 31 years, beginning the decline in the total yearend prison population. Admissions to state and federal prisons declined by 118,900 offenders (down 16.3%) between 2009 and 2012. In 2012, the number of admissions (609,800) was the lowest since 1999, representing a 9.2% decline (down 61,800 offenders) from 2011.

This report describes changes in the types of state prison admissions and releases between 1991 and 2011. Changes over time in the total yearend prison population are influenced by changes in the number of state prisoners who make up 87% of the total prison population. The report also discusses how these changes influence sex, race, Hispanic origin, offense, and sentence length distributions. The statistics in this report are based on the Bureau of Justice Statistics' (BJS) National Prisoner Statistics (NPS) Program, National Corrections Reporting Program, and the 1991 and 2004 surveys of state prison inmates.

FIGURE 1
Sentenced state and federal prison admissions and releases and yearend sentenced prison population, 1978–2012

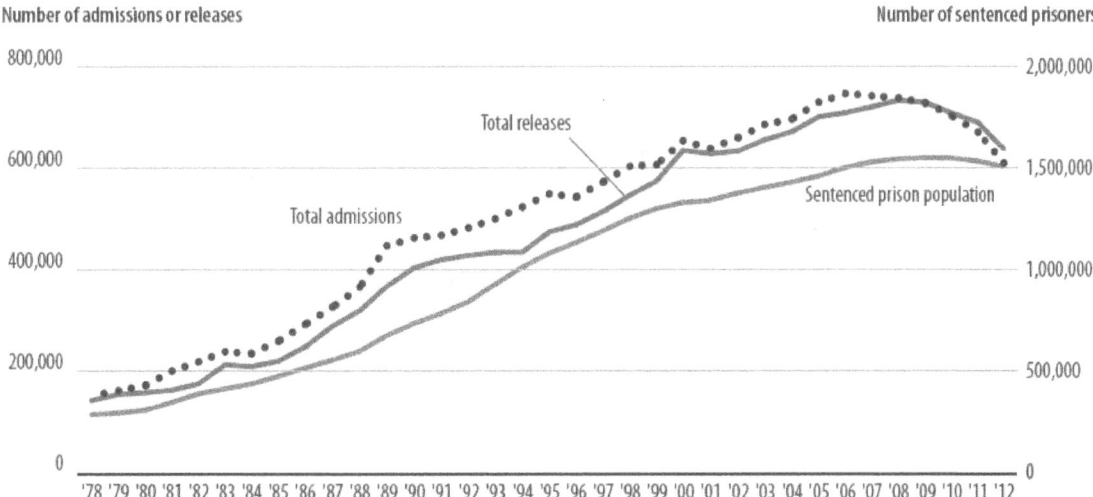

Note: Counts based on prisoners with a sentence of more than 1 year. Excludes transfers, escapes, and those absent without leave (AWOL). Includes other conditional release violators, returns from appeal or bond, and other admissions. Missing data were imputed for Illinois and Nevada (2012) and the Federal Bureau of Prisons (1990–1992). See *Methodology.*
Source: Bureau of Justice Statistics, National Prisoner Statistics Program, 1978–2012.

BJS

HIGHLIGHTS

- In 2012, the number of admissions to state and federal prison in the United States was 609,800 offenders, the lowest number since 1999.

- The number of releases from U.S. prisons in 2012 (637,400) exceeded that of admissions for the fourth consecutive year, contributing to the decline in the total U.S. prison population.

- In 2011, the majority of state prisoners in 2011 (53%) were serving time for violent offenses.

- New court commitments made up 82% of state admissions in 1978, 57% in 2000, and 71% in 2012.

- New court commitments to state prisons for drug offenders decreased 22% between 2006 and 2011, while parole violation admissions decreased 31%.

- Between 1991 and 2011, new court commitments of females to state prison for violent offenses increased 83%, from 4,800 in 1991 to 8,700 in 2011.

- Drug offenses accounted for 24% of new court admissions of black inmates in 2011, a decrease from a range of 35% to 38% from 1991 to 2006.

- Since 1991, the proportion of newly admitted violent offenders receiving prison sentences of less than 5 years has increased.

- California's Public Safety Realignment policy drove the decrease in the total number of admissions to California state prisons, as well as a decline in the proportion of admissions to California state prisons for parole violation (from 65% in 2010 to 23% in 2012).

- Prisoners age 44 and younger accounted for 80% of prison admissions, 77% of releases, and 72% of the yearend population in 2012.

- The number of prisoners sentenced to more than 1 year under state or federal correctional authorities in 2012 was 1,511,500, down from 1,538,800 at yearend 2011.

The drop in state prison admissions drove the overall decline in U.S. prison admissions in 2012

Admissions to U.S. prisons in 2012 declined by 61,800 offenders (9.2%) from 2011, the sixth year in which the number of admissions has decreased. Admissions declined from a high of 747,000 in 2006 to 609,800 in 2012 (table 1). Both state departments of corrections and the Federal Bureau of Prisons admitted fewer inmates in 2012 than in 2011, although the decline in admissions to state prisons (down 57,100) accounted for 92% of the total decrease. The number of admissions to state prisons in 2012 (553,800) is the lowest since 1997. The highest number of admissions to federal prisons occurred in 2011 (60,600 admissions). In 2012, federal prison admissions decreased by 4,700 admissions or 7.7%.

Admissions or entries to prison for violating conditional release from prison, typically referred to as parole violation admissions (which also include new crimes committed while serving a term of parole), represented 16% of all state prison admissions and 10% of federal prison admissions in 1978. However, this type of admission increased over the following years.

Admissions for new crimes (82% of all state admissions in 1978) reached a low of 57% in 2000 before rebounding to 65% in 2011. New court commitments accounted for 71% of all state and 92% of federal prison entries in 2012. While the overall number of new court commitments to state prisons declined by 1.3% between 2011 and 2012, the proportion of this type of admissions increased due to a 26% decrease in the number of parole violation admissions.

About 8% (4,700 prisoners) of federal prison admissions in 2012 were prisoners returned for violating their conditional release. There were 52,400 fewer admissions due to parole violation to state prisons in 2012 than in 2011 (down 26%). Parole violation admissions accounted for 27% of the total state prison entries, down from 33% in 2011. This decrease can be attributed to the large decline in parole violation admissions in California, from 60,300 in 2011 to 8,000 in 2012. Overall, admissions to California prisons declined by 65% between 2011 and 2012, while entries on parole violations decreased by 87% (appendix table 1).

TABLE 1
Sentenced state and federal prison admissions, by type of admission, 1978–2012

Year	All admissions[a]			New court commitments			Parole violations[b]		
	Total	Federal	State	Total	Federal	State	Total	Federal	State
1978	152,039	14,724	137,315	126,121	13,247	112,874	23,844	1,429	22,415
1979	161,280	14,120	147,160	131,057	12,619	118,438	25,668	1,454	24,214
1980	171,884	12,598	159,286	142,122	10,907	131,215	28,817	1,640	27,177
1981	199,943	12,830	187,113	160,272	11,086	149,186	35,674	1,709	33,965
1982	218,087	14,818	203,269	177,109	12,461	164,648	39,003	2,317	36,686
1983	237,925	16,745	221,180	187,408	14,119	173,289	45,568	2,583	42,985
1984	234,293	16,013	218,280	180,418	13,491	166,927	52,007	2,475	49,532
1985	258,514	17,916	240,598	198,499	15,368	183,131	58,694	2,502	56,192
1986	291,903	18,501	273,402	219,382	16,067	203,315	71,184	2,401	68,783
1987	326,228	18,709	307,519	241,887	16,260	225,627	82,959	2,435	80,524
1988	365,724	18,696	347,028	261,242	15,932	245,310	101,354	2,744	98,610
1989	447,388	23,491	423,897	316,215	18,388	297,827	122,156	1,611	120,545
1990[c]	462,500	/	460,739	328,300	/	323,069	133,600	/	133,870
1991[c]	468,000	/	466,285	322,500	/	317,237	141,800	/	142,100
1992[c]	482,400	/	480,676	339,600	/	334,301	141,700	/	141,961
1993	500,335	25,235	475,100	341,722	23,653	318,069	147,712	1,346	146,366
1994	523,577	27,271	496,306	345,035	23,956	321,079	170,974	3,146	167,828
1995	549,313	27,337	521,976	361,464	23,972	337,492	178,641	2,915	175,726
1996	542,863	30,239	512,624	353,893	27,346	326,547	175,311	2,672	172,639
1997	572,281	33,906	538,375	365,085	30,560	334,525	189,765	3,106	186,659
1998	603,510	38,219	565,291	381,646	34,376	347,270	209,782	3,630	206,152
1999	606,728	41,972	564,756	375,796	37,455	338,341	202,163	4,292	197,871
2000	654,534	43,732	610,802	389,734	39,303	350,431	207,755	4,186	203,569
2001	638,978	45,140	593,838	405,422	40,193	365,229	220,064	4,720	215,344
2002	660,576	48,144	612,432	433,959	42,303	391,656	213,455	5,600	207,855
2003	686,471	52,288	634,183	445,556	45,713	399,843	205,062	6,357	198,705
2004	697,066	52,982	644,084	457,096	45,796	411,300	226,211	7,178	219,033
2005	730,141	56,057	674,084	470,149	48,723	421,426	239,560	7,331	232,229
2006	747,031	57,495	689,536	492,315	50,204	442,111	246,571	7,286	239,285
2007	742,875	53,618	689,257	479,710	48,691	431,019	252,775	4,924	247,851
2008	738,631	53,662	684,969	477,100	49,270	427,830	253,035	4,390	248,645
2009	728,686	56,153	672,533	474,997	51,524	423,473	242,347	4,628	237,719
2010	703,798	54,121	649,677	458,360	49,515	408,845	231,917	4,606	227,311
2011[d]	671,551	60,634	610,917	454,526	55,817	398,709	205,297	4,816	200,481
2012[d,e]	609,781	55,938	553,843	444,591	51,241	393,350	152,780	4,696	148,084

/Not reported.

[a]Counts based on prisoners with a sentence of more than 1 year. Excludes transfers, escapes, and those absent without leave (AWOL). Totals for all admissions include other conditional release violations, returns from appeal or bond, and other admissions. See *Methodology*.

[b]Includes all conditional release violators returned to prison for either violations of conditions of release or for new crimes.

[c]The Federal Bureau of Prisons did not report admission data. National totals include an imputed count for BOP admissions.

[d]Alaska did not report type of admission. State and national totals for all admissions include Alaska counts, but totals for admission types do not.

[e]Missing 2012 data were imputed for Illinois and Nevada.

Source: Bureau of Justice Statistics, National Prisoner Statistics Program, 1978–2012.

Releases from state prison in 2012 exceeded admissions for the fourth consecutive year, contributing to the decline in the total prison population

Although the number of releases or exits from U.S. prisons declined 7.7% between 2011 and 2012, releases exceeded the number of prison admissions (table 2). Total U.S. and state prison releases have outpaced admissions since 2009. The decline in releases from state prison offset the increase in exits from federal prison. State prisons released 54,500 fewer inmates in 2012 than in 2011. However, 27 states had an increase in the number of releases from 2011 to 2012, led by Colorado (up 17%), Hawaii and Massachusetts (up 16% each), Idaho (up 13%), and Nebraska (up 12%) (appendix table 1).

The number of releases from California state prisons declined by 62,000 offenders (down 57%), from 109,500 in 2011 to 47,500 in 2012. Twenty-three other states released fewer inmates from prison in 2012 compared to 2011, including New Hampshire (down 17%), Arkansas (down 13%), Oklahoma (down 10%), Nevada (down 9%), and Georgia and Michigan (down 8% each).

TABLE 2
Sentenced state and federal prison releases, by type of release, 1978–2012

Year	All releases[a]			Conditional releases[b]			Unconditional releases[c]		
	Total	Federal	State	Total	Federal	State	Total	Federal	State
1978	142,033	17,361	124,672	107,691	9,651	98,040	25,902	4,146	21,756
1979	154,277	18,518	135,759	117,135	10,442	106,693	26,754	4,493	22,261
1980	157,604	14,748	142,856	122,952	8,252	114,700	25,915	3,647	22,268
1981	162,294	11,715	150,579	124,415	6,431	117,984	27,901	3,396	24,505
1982	174,808	13,373	161,435	140,179	7,086	133,093	28,913	4,862	24,051
1983	212,302	14,415	197,887	166,345	8,151	158,194	38,307	5,264	33,043
1984	208,608	15,024	193,584	166,417	8,933	157,484	39,192	5,177	34,015
1985	219,310	13,410	205,900	174,916	8,748	166,168	41,915	4,188	37,727
1986	247,619	15,115	232,504	202,530	10,118	192,412	42,832	4,572	38,260
1987	288,781	16,012	272,769	232,871	11,358	221,513	53,253	4,260	48,993
1988	318,889	15,302	303,587	253,651	9,511	244,140	62,675	5,437	57,238
1989	367,388	18,104	349,284	302,327	13,136	289,191	62,107	4,864	57,243
1990[d]	404,000	/	403,777	337,000	/	339,439	57,900	/	55,243
1991[d]	420,000	/	419,831	351,300	/	353,774	58,200	/	55,579
1992[d]	428,300	/	428,110	355,300	/	357,731	61,100	/	58,425
1993	434,082	18,676	415,406	355,773	5,742	350,031	69,636	12,801	56,835
1994	434,766	21,062	413,704	353,020	4,790	348,230	72,836	15,986	56,850
1995	474,296	22,292	452,004	374,483	3,747	370,736	88,081	18,054	70,027
1996	488,748	24,647	464,101	369,808	3,176	366,632	103,435	19,699	83,736
1997	514,322	27,280	487,042	386,076	2,445	383,631	109,896	22,294	87,602
1998	546,616	29,239	517,377	406,050	2,148	403,902	126,086	23,939	102,147
1999	574,624	31,816	542,808	420,306	1,919	418,387	128,923	26,089	102,834
2000	635,094	35,259	599,835	426,617	1,991	424,626	148,336	29,180	119,156
2001	628,626	38,370	590,256	438,449	2,234	436,215	162,007	31,715	130,292
2002	633,947	42,339	591,608	443,996	3,154	440,842	161,293	33,904	127,389
2003	656,574	44,135	612,439	444,771	2,603	442,168	163,607	36,221	127,386
2004	672,202	46,624	625,578	483,215	2,488	480,727	166,862	43,715	123,147
2005	701,632	48,323	653,309	497,475	2,105	495,370	179,651	45,708	133,943
2006	709,874	47,920	661,954	499,950	1,746	498,204	193,720	45,749	147,971
2007	721,161	48,764	672,397	505,726	1,545	504,181	199,393	46,804	152,589
2008	734,144	52,348	681,796	505,350	1,225	504,125	216,036	50,708	165,328
2009	729,749	50,720	679,029	505,504	1,479	504,025	211,324	49,208	162,116
2,010	708,677	52,487	656,190	494,249	962	493,287	202,499	51,110	151,389
2011[e]	691,072	55,239	635,833	474,681	649	474,032	202,602	54,163	148,439
2012[e,f]	637,411	56,037	581,374	408,186	591	407,595	213,204	55,079	158,125

/Not reported.

[a]Counts based on prisoners with a sentence of more than 1 year. Excludes transfers, escapes, and those absent without leave (AWOL). Totals for all releases include deaths, releases to appeal or bond, and other releases. See *Methodology*.

[b]Includes releases to probation, supervised mandatory releases, and other unspecified conditional releases.

[c]Includes expirations of sentence, commutations, and other unconditional releases.

[d]The Federal Bureau of Prisons did not report release data. National totals include an imputed count for BOP releases.

[e]Alaska did not report type of release. State and national totals for all releases include Alaska counts, but totals for release types do not.

[f]Missing 2012 data were imputed for Illinois and Nevada.

Source: Bureau of Justice Statistics, National Prisoner Statistics Program, 1978–2012.

Releases from federal prisons increased by more than 1% in 2012, continuing a trend that started in 2009. The BOP released 56,000 inmates in 2012, which exceeded admissions by 100 inmates. This was the first year in more than a decade in which the federal system released more inmates than it admitted.

Conditional releases, including supervised mandatory releases, discretionary parole, and shock probation, continued a decline that started in 2009, decreasing 14% between 2011 and 2012. Federal prisons released 9% fewer inmates on conditional status in 2012 than in 2011 due to the decline in federal prison inmates sentenced before the Sentencing Reform Act of 1984, which abolished parole for federal prisoners. Conditional releases accounted for 1% of exits from federal prisons in 2012, compared to 70% of state prison releases. Since 1978, conditional releases accounted for 70% to 84% of state prison releases.

In comparison, the number of unconditional releases increased in both state and federal prison systems. State prisons had 6.5% (or 9,700) more unconditional releases in 2012 than in 2011, while these exits increased by 1.7% (or 900 inmates) in the federal system. In 2011, California released 13,700 inmates without conditions, which increased to about 29,500 offenders in 2012. Nationally, unconditional prison releases accounted for 33% of all exits, up from 29% in 2011.

Violent offenders accounted for a larger proportion of the state prison population between 1991 and 2011

In 1991, 45% of all state prisoners—or an estimated 327,000 offenders—were sentenced to more than 1 year for violent offenses (table 3). On December 31, 2006 (the year in which admissions to state prisons reached their peak), 50% of all sentenced prisoners in custody of state correctional authorities were violent offenders. In 2011 (the most recent year for which state prison offense data are available), more than 53% (or an estimated 718,000 offenders) of the yearend population was serving a sentence for a violent crime. While robbery was the most common offense across the 20-year period, the proportion of violent offenders convicted for murder or any sexual assault increased over time. Property offenders (250,000 prisoners or 19% of all state prisoners) exceeded the number of drug offenders in custody in 2011 (223,000 inmates, or 17% of the inmate population).

TABLE 3

Estimated percent of sentenced prisoners under state jurisdiction, by most serious offense, December 31, 1991, 2001, 2006, and 2011

Most serious offense	1991	2001	2006	2011
Total	100%	100%	100%	100%
Violent	44.6%	50.6%	50.4%	53.5%
Murder[a]	10.8	12.1	11.4	12.6
Negligent manslaughter	2.1	1.4	1.4	1.5
Rape/sexual assault	8.2	11.2	11.8	12.4
Robbery	13.9	13.5	13.2	13.7
Assault	7.9	9.7	9.9	10.3
Other violent	1.7	2.7	2.7	2.9
Property	25.3%	20.6%	19.6%	18.6%
Burglary	11.2	10.3	9.6	9.9
Larceny	5.8	4.0	3.4	3.2
Motor vehicle theft	1.9	1.4	1.6	1.1
Fraud	3.9	2.5	2.7	2.2
Other property	2.5	2.4	2.3	2.2
Drug	23.0%	21.0%	20.0%	16.6%
Possession	8.2	4.6	5.3	4.1
Other drug[b]	14.8	16.4	14.7	12.5
Public order[c]	6.6%	7.2%	9.4%	10.6%
Other/unspecified[d]	0.4%	0.6%	0.6%	0.7%
Number of sentenced prisoners	732,916	1,208,708	1,331,065	1,341,797

Note: Counts based on prisoners under state jurisdiction on December 31 with a sentence of more than 1 year. Detail may not sum to total due to rounding and missing offense data. Estimates may vary from those previously published due to differences in methodology. Sentenced prisoner totals from National Prisoner Statistics Program. Offense distribution based on National Corrections Reporting Program administrative data. See *Methodology*.

[a]Includes nonnegligent manslaughter.
[b]Includes drug trafficking.
[c]Includes weapons, drunk driving, and court offenses; habitual offender sanctions; commercialized vice, morals, and decency offenses; and liquor law violations and other public order offenses.
[d]Includes juvenile offenses and other unspecified offense categories.

Sources: Bureau of Justice Statistics, National Prisoner Statistics Program, 1991, 2001, 2006, and 2011; National Corrections Reporting Program, 2001, 2006, and 2011;and Survey of Inmates in State Correctional Facilities, 1991.

An increase in the number of admissions to state prisons for violent offenses contributed to the growth of these sentenced inmates in the yearend prison population. Fewer violent offenders than property and drug offenders were admitted in 1991, 2001, and 2006 (table 4), but by 2011, the estimated proportion of admissions for violent and property offenses was roughly equal. There were 78,600 fewer total admissions in 2011 than in 2006, and 65% of this decline (or an estimated 51,000 persons) was due to fewer admissions for drug crimes. A drop in the number of persons sentenced for drug crimes other than possession accounted for the majority (66%, or an estimated 33,600 persons) of the decrease in admissions for drug crimes between 2006 and 2011.

TABLE 4

Estimated state prison admissions, by most serious offense, 1991, 2001, 2006, and 2011

Most serious offense	1991	2001	2006	2011
Total	100%	100%	100%	100%
Violent	26.9%	27.3%	26.1%	29.1%
Murder[a]	2.6	2.1	1.7	2.0
Negligent manslaughter	1.0	0.8	0.7	0.7
Rape/sexual assault	4.9	5.2	5.1	5.4
Robbery	10.5	8.5	7.0	8.0
Assault	6.7	8.7	9.3	10.6
Other violent	1.1	2.1	2.3	2.4
Property	35.4%	29.4%	29.1%	29.0%
Burglary	16.1	11.4	10.7	12.4
Larceny	9.4	7.5	6.6	6.1
Motor vehicle theft	3.0	2.7	3.4	2.6
Fraud	3.9	4.2	4.7	3.9
Other property	2.9	3.6	3.7	4.0
Drug	28.3%	32.1%	29.9%	25.4%
Possession	7.0	8.9	9.7	8.0
Other drug[b]	21.3	23.3	20.2	17.3
Public order[c]	7.8%	10.6%	14.4%	15.8%
Other/unspecified[d]	1.6%	0.5%	0.6%	0.8%
Number of admissions	466,285	593,838	689,536	610,917

Note: Counts based on prisoners with a sentence of more than 1 year admitted to state prison. Excludes transfers, escapes, and those absent without leave (AWOL). Detail may not sum to total due to rounding and missing offense data. Admission totals from National Prisoner Statistics Program. Offense distribution based on National Corrections Reporting Program administrative data. See *Methodology*. Estimates may vary from those previously published due to differences in methodology.

[a]Includes nonnegligent manslaughter.

[b]Includes drug trafficking.

[c]Includes weapons, drunk driving, and court offenses; habitual offender sanctions; commercialized vice, morals, and decency offenses; and liquor law violations and other public order offenses.

[d]Includes juvenile offenses and other unspecified offense categories.

Sources: Bureau of Justice Statistics, National Prisoner Statistics Program and National Corrections Reporting Program, 1991, 2001, 2006, and 2011.

Between 1991 and 2011, changes in state prison admission types were associated with changes in the offense distributions

As the distribution of types of admissions to state prison changed over time, so did the demographic and offense compositions of admitted prisoners. In 1991, new court commitments were almost equally distributed between violent, property, and drug offenses, while parole violation admissions of property offenders were almost twice the number of admissions for violent crimes or drug offenses (table 5). By 2001, the distribution between the three offense categories for parole violation admissions was more balanced, and drug offenders represented the largest proportion of both new court commitments and parole violation admissions.

The number of new admissions and readmissions for violent offenses increased between 1991 and 2006, but only due to the overall growth in state prison admissions. The proportion of violent offenders among new court commitment and parole violation admissions was stable until each increased by about 3% in 2011.

New court commitments of individuals committing drug offenses other than possession, a category that includes drug trafficking, decreased by 19% (or 16,300 inmates) between 2006 and 2011. The number of persons newly admitted to prison on drug possession sentences experienced a 27% decline during the same period, with an estimated 11,300 fewer new admissions. Parole violation admissions for drug offenders decreased 31% or 23,300 fewer readmissions.

TABLE 5
Estimated state prison admissions, by type of admission and most serious offense, 1991, 2001, 2006, and 2011

Most serious offense[a]	1991		2001		2006		2011	
	New court commitment	Parole violation[a]	New court commitment	Parole violation[a]	New court commitment	Parole violation[a]	New court commitment	Parole violation[a]
Total	100%	100%	100%	100%	100%	100%	100%	100%
Violent	28.7%	23.7%	29.4%	23.9%	27.3%	24.1%	30.0%	27.4%
Murder[b]	3.0	1.7	2.5	1.3	2.0	1.1	2.4	1.2
Negligent manslaughter	1.3	0.5	1.0	0.4	0.8	0.4	0.8	0.3
Rape/sexual assault	5.6	3.6	6.3	3.4	5.7	3.9	5.7	4.8
Robbery	9.9	11.6	8.1	9.2	6.8	7.4	7.9	8.4
Assault	7.5	5.5	9.2	7.9	9.5	9.1	10.7	10.5
Other violent	1.4	0.7	2.3	1.8	2.4	2.1	2.5	2.2
Property	31.4%	42.4%	27.4%	32.5%	26.9%	33.3%	27.5%	32.4%
Burglary	13.5	20.8	10.4	12.9	9.9	12.4	12.1	13.1
Larceny	8.1	11.7	6.6	8.8	6.1	7.4	5.9	6.6
Motor vehicle theft	2.4	4.1	2.0	3.9	2.4	5.4	1.7	4.9
Fraud	3.8	4.1	4.7	3.3	4.9	4.1	4.1	3.4
Other property	3.6	1.8	3.7	3.5	3.5	4.0	3.8	4.4
Drug	29.9%	25.5%	30.5%	35.1%	28.8%	31.7%	24.9%	26.2%
Possession	6.9	7.0	8.7	9.1	9.6	9.7	7.8	8.7
Other drug[c]	23.0	18.5	21.8	26.0	19.2	22.0	17.2	17.5
Public order[d]	8.9%	6.1%	12.1%	8.0%	16.4%	10.3%	16.8%	13.2%
Other/unspecified[e]	1.1%	2.3%	0.6%	0.5%	0.6%	0.6%	0.8%	0.8%
Number of admissions	317,237	142,100	365,229	215,344	442,111	239,285	398,709	200,481

Note: Based on prisoners with a sentence of more than 1 year admitted to state prison on a new court commitment or on a conditional release violation, either for a release condition violation or for a new crime. Detail may not sum to total due to rounding and missing offense data. Admission totals from National Prisoner Statistics Program. Offense distribution based on National Corrections Reporting Program administrative data. See *Methodology*. Estimates may vary from those previously published due to differences in methodology.

[a]For parole violation admissions, most serious offense refers to the original offense for which an inmate was sentenced, not the incident causing the parole revocation.

[b]Includes nonnegligent manslaughter.

[c]Includes drug trafficking.

[d]Includes weapons, drunk driving, and court offenses; habitual offender sanctions; commercialized vice, morals, and decency offenses; and liquor law violations and other public order offenses.

[e]Includes juvenile offenses and other unspecified offense categories.

Sources: Bureau of Justice Statistics, National Prisoner Statistics Program and National Corrections Reporting Program, 1991, 2001, 2006, and 2011.

The number of females admitted on new court commitments for violent offenses in 2011 increased by 2% from 2006 and by 83% from 1991

Between 1991 and 2006, the number of new court commitments to state prison for violent offenses increased by 30% for males and 79% for females, although the proportion of violent crime new court commitments remained roughly the same (table 6). In 2011, the proportion of violent offenders among all new court commitments increased for both males and females. However, because of the decrease in overall admissions between 2006 and 2011, about 1,500 fewer males were admitted to state prison for violent crimes, while the number of females increased by 180 violent offenders. Over the 20-year period, the number of females admitted for violent offenses on new court commitments increased 83%, from 4,800 in 1991 to 8,700 in 2011.

While the proportion of property crime offenders among new court commitments decreased among males between 1991 and 2006, the number of male offenders sentenced for these crimes increased due to the overall growth in state prison admissions. In 2006, 19,600 females entered prison for property crimes compared to 10,300 in 1991, and 17,100 in 2011. New admissions for public order offenses—including weapons and drunk driving offenses, habitual offender sanctions, and vice crimes—increased by about 39,100 for male inmates between 1991 and 2006, the largest absolute change in the number of admissions. Among the most common public order offenses resulting in a new court commitment to prison, weapons offenses increased 157% between 1991 and 2011, driving while under the influence grew 61%, and court offenses (including perjury, failure to appear, bond jumping, and tampering) increased 751% (detailed breakdown of offense categories not shown). Obstruction of law enforcement grew 226% over the same period, and admissions of habitual offenders increased 311%.

TABLE 6
Estimated new court commitments to state prison, by sex and most serious offense, 1991, 2001, 2006, and 2011

Most serious offense	1991		2001		2006		2011	
	Male	Female	Male	Female	Male	Female	Male	Female
Total	100%	100%	100%	100%	100%	100%	100%	100%
Violent	29.9%	16.5%	30.8%	17.2%	28.9%	15.8%	31.5%	18.4%
Murder[a]	3.1	2.5	2.6	2.0	2.1	1.4	2.4	1.7
Negligent manslaughter	1.2	1.9	0.9	1.4	0.8	0.9	0.8	1.1
Rape/sexual assault	6.1	0.6	6.9	0.9	6.4	0.8	6.3	1.0
Robbery	10.4	5.2	8.6	4.4	7.2	4.0	8.3	4.9
Assault	7.7	5.1	9.5	6.0	10.0	6.4	11.2	6.9
Other violent	1.4	1.3	2.3	2.5	2.4	2.4	2.4	2.8
Property	31.0%	35.7%	26.3%	36.8%	25.6%	36.2%	26.4%	36.0%
Burglary	14.3	5.2	10.9	5.8	10.4	6.1	12.6	8.0
Larceny	7.4	15.3	6.0	12.0	5.5	10.5	5.3	10.6
Motor vehicle theft	2.6	0.9	2.1	1.3	2.5	2.2	1.7	1.5
Fraud	3.1	11.8	3.6	14.7	3.6	14.2	3.1	11.7
Other property	3.7	2.5	3.7	3.1	3.5	3.2	3.7	4.1
Drug	28.8%	40.9%	29.7%	37.3%	28.1%	34.2%	23.9%	32.5%
Possession	6.7	9.6	8.4	11.7	9.2	12.7	7.2	11.7
Other drug[b]	22.2	31.3	21.3	25.6	18.9	21.5	16.7	20.8
Public order[c]	9.2%	5.6%	12.6%	8.0%	16.9%	13.1%	17.4%	12.0%
Other/unspecified[d]	1.1%	1.4%	0.5%	0.7%	0.5%	0.8%	0.7%	1.1%
Number of new court commitments	288,408	28,829	325,801	39,428	388,081	54,030	351,326	47,383

Note: Based on prisoners with a sentence of more than 1 year admitted to state prison on a new court commitment. Detail may not sum to total due to rounding and missing offense data. Admission totals from National Prisoner Statistics Program. Offense distribution based on National Corrections Reporting Program administrative data. See *Methodology*. Estimates may vary from those previously published due to differences in methodology.
[a]Includes nonnegligent manslaughter.
[b]Includes drug trafficking.
[c]Includes weapons, drunk driving, and court offenses; habitual offender sanctions; commercialized vice, morals, and decency offenses; and liquor law violations and other public order offenses.
[d]Includes juvenile offenses and other unspecified offense categories.
Sources: Bureau of Justice Statistics, National Prisoner Statistics Program and National Corrections Reporting Program, 1991, 2001, 2006, and 2011.

In 2001, 34% of male readmissions to state prison and 47% of female readmissions were sentenced drug offenders returning on parole violations (table 7). These proportions declined to 26% of males and 33% of females in 2011. For both males and females, the proportion of readmissions to state prison for drug possession offenders increased in 2006 and then decreased in 2011 to levels comparable to those in 2001.

TABLE 7
Estimated parole violation admissions to state prison, by sex and most serious offense, 1991, 2001, 2006, and 2011

Most serious offense[a]	1991		2001		2006		2011	
	Male	Female	Male	Female	Male	Female	Male	Female
Total	100%	100%	100%	100%	100%	100%	100%	100%
Violent	24.5%	14.0%	25.0%	11.6%	25.2%	12.3%	28.4%	14.6%
Murder[b]	1.8	1.1	1.3	0.7	1.2	0.5	1.2	0.4
Negligent manslaughter	0.5	0.5	0.4	0.3	0.4	0.5	0.3	0.3
Rape/sexual assault	3.9	0.3	3.7	0.3	4.2	0.6	5.1	0.8
Robbery	11.9	7.5	9.6	4.9	7.7	4.0	8.7	5.0
Assault	5.6	4.0	8.3	3.9	9.5	4.6	10.8	6.4
Other violent	0.7	0.6	1.8	1.5	2.1	2.2	2.2	1.7
Property	42.2%	45.2%	32.2%	36.0%	32.6%	40.8%	31.6%	42.5%
Burglary	21.7	9.2	13.4	7.6	12.7	8.4	13.4	9.9
Larceny	10.9	20.9	8.3	14.5	7.0	11.5	6.2	10.8
Motor vehicle theft	4.3	1.5	4.1	2.2	5.5	4.8	4.9	4.5
Fraud	3.4	12.5	2.7	9.2	3.4	12.1	2.8	11.6
Other property	1.9	1.1	3.6	2.6	4.0	4.0	4.3	5.7
Drug	24.7%	35.8%	34.1%	46.6%	31.0%	39.5%	25.7%	33.2%
Possession	6.6	11.3	8.9	11.6	9.4	13.1	8.5	11.6
Other drug[c]	18.1	24.5	25.2	35.0	21.6	26.4	17.2	21.6
Public order[d]	6.3%	3.3%	8.2%	5.2%	10.7%	6.7%	13.5%	8.7%
Other/unspecified[e]	2.3%	1.7%	0.5%	0.5%	0.6%	0.8%	0.8%	1.0%
Number of parole violation admissions	132,288	9,812	197,537	17,807	218,488	20,797	184,513	15,968

Note: Based on prisoners with a sentence of more than 1 year returned to state prison on all conditional release violations for either violations of conditions of release, or for new crimes. Detail may not sum to total due to rounding and missing offense data. Admission totals from National Prisoner Statistics Program. Offense distribution based on National Corrections Reporting Program administrative data. See *Methodology*. Estimates may vary from those previously published due to differences in methodology.
[a]For parole violation admissions, most serious offense refers to the original offense for which an inmate was sentenced, not the incident causing the parole revocation.
[b]Includes nonnegligent manslaughter.
[c]Includes drug trafficking.
[d]Includes weapons, drunk driving, and court offenses; habitual offender sanctions; commercialized vice, morals, and decency offenses; and liquor law violations and other public order offenses.
[e]Includes juvenile offenses and other unspecified offense categories.
Sources: Bureau of Justice Statistics, National Prisoner Statistics Program and National Corrections Reporting Program, 1991, 2001, 2006, and 2011.

Among new court commitments to state prison, more than a third each of black and Hispanic offenders, and a quarter of white offenders were convicted of a violent offense

In 2011, 34% of non-Hispanic black offenders (54,000 admissions) and 36% of Hispanic offenders (25,000 admissions) entering state prison on new court commitments had committed violent offenses (table 8). For black offenders, this represented an increase over 1991, 2001, and 2006, when less than 30% of new admissions were for violent crimes. New court commitments for non-Hispanic white offenders convicted of violent crimes represented 25% (37,000 offenders) of all new admissions of white offenders in 2011.

TABLE 8
Estimated new court commitments to state prison, by race, Hispanic origin, and most serious offense, 1991, 2001, 2006, and 2011

Most serious offense	1991[a] White	1991[a] Black	2001[b] White[c]	2001[b] Black[c]	2001[b] Hispanic	2006[b] White[c]	2006[b] Black[c]	2006[b] Hispanic	2011[b] White[c]	2011[b] Black[c]	2011[b] Hispanic
Total	100%	100%	100%	100%	100%	100%	100%	100%	100%	100%	100%
Violent	26.7%	28.7%	27.7%	28.8%	34.1%	23.9%	29.0%	32.2%	25.3%	34.4%	35.7%
Murder[d]	2.5	2.9	1.9	2.8	3.3	1.3	2.3	2.5	1.4	2.8	3.2
Negligent manslaughter	1.8	1.1	1.1	0.7	0.9	0.9	0.5	0.8	0.9	0.6	0.7
Rape/sexual assault	8.6	3.1	8.9	3.7	6.9	7.0	3.7	6.4	6.7	3.7	7.0
Robbery	5.7	13.2	4.8	10.5	8.2	3.9	9.9	7.4	4.5	12.5	8.1
Assault	6.4	7.4	8.5	9.1	11.9	8.3	10.3	12.0	9.2	12.2	13.5
Other violent	1.8	1.1	2.5	2.0	2.9	2.6	2.3	3.1	2.6	2.5	3.2
Property	40.8%	26.4%	34.1%	24.2%	19.9%	33.3%	22.7%	22.8%	33.5%	24.6%	21.2%
Burglary	17.7	11.4	13.1	9.0	8.3	11.9	8.8	9.1	13.9	12.3	10.5
Larceny	9.6	7.0	7.6	6.7	4.0	7.6	5.9	4.2	7.4	5.2	4.0
Motor vehicle theft	3.1	2.1	2.3	1.8	3.1	2.6	1.4	4.5	1.9	1.0	2.3
Fraud	6.0	3.1	6.5	4.3	1.7	6.9	4.2	2.4	5.2	3.6	2.0
Other property	4.4	2.7	4.5	2.5	2.8	4.4	2.3	2.6	5.1	2.5	2.3
Drug	19.3%	38.5%	23.1%	36.8%	36.4%	23.8%	35.0%	29.5%	23.1%	24.3%	25.5%
Possession	5.3	11.2	8.5	10.6	8.1	9.4	11.3	10.9	8.2	7.4	9.5
Other drug[e]	14.0	27.3	14.6	26.2	28.2	14.4	23.7	18.6	15.0	16.9	16.0
Public order[f]	11.4%	5.4%	15.1%	10.2%	9.7%	19.0%	13.4%	15.5%	18.0%	16.7%	17.6%
Other/unspecified[g]	1.8%	1.0%	0.6%	0.3%	0.7%	0.7%	0.4%	0.4%	1.1%	0.7%	0.4%
Number of new court commitments	149,488	146,833	133,442	143,775	63,992	162,084	173,614	77,274	146,054	156,661	69,728

Note: Based on prisoners with a sentence of more than 1 year admitted to state prison on a new court commitment. Detail may not sum to total due to rounding, missing offense data, and racial categories not shown. Admission totals from National Prisoner Statistics Program. Offense distribution based on National Corrections Reporting Program administrative data. See *Methodology*. Estimates may vary from those previously published due to differences in methodology.

[a]Race and Hispanic origin data are weighted to represent the race/ethnicity distribution from the 1991 Survey of Inmates in State Correctional Facilities. See *Methodology*. The U.S. Office of Management and Budget published guidelines on the collection and reporting of Hispanic origin in 1997 (http://www.whitehouse.gov/omb/fedreg_1997standards/) and few states collected ethnicity data in 1991. Persons of Hispanic or Latino origin are included in the White and Black categories.

[b]Race and Hispanic origin data are weighted to represent the race/ethnicity distribution from the 2004 Survey of Inmates in State Correctional Facilities. See *Methodology*.

[c]Excludes persons of Hispanic or Latino origin and persons of two or more races.

[d]Includes nonnegligent manslaughter.

[e]Includes drug trafficking.

[f]Includes weapons, drunk driving, and court offenses; habitual offender sanctions; commercialized vice, morals, and decency offenses; and liquor law violations and other public order offenses.

[g]Includes juvenile offenses and other unspecified offense categories.

Sources: Bureau of Justice Statistics, National Prisoner Statistics Program and National Corrections Reporting Program, 1991, 2001, 2006, and 2011; and Survey of Inmates in State Correctional Facilities, 1991 and 2004.

A third of whites imprisoned for new offenses in 2011 were convicted for property offenses (49,000), compared to 25% of blacks (38,600) and 21% of Hispanics (15,000). In 1991, 38% of all blacks admitted to state prison were serving time for new drug offenses. In 2011, only 24% of all blacks were admitted for drug crimes.

Blacks accounted for 47% of new court commitments for violent offenses in 2011, compared to 44% in 2006 and 41% in 2001. Less than a third of inmates newly committed to state prison for violent offenses in 2011 were white (32%), down from 37% in 2001. The racial and Hispanic origin of new admissions for murder and nonnegligent manslaughter between 2001 and 2011 showed a decrease among whites (from 29% in 2001 to 24% in 2011), and increases among blacks (from 46% in 2001 to 51% in 2011) and Hispanics (from

24% in 2001 to 26% in 2011). Among newly sentenced drug offenders, blacks showed a large decline, from 49% of all new court commitment admissions for drug crimes in 2001 to 42% in 2011. In comparison, whites increased from 29% of newly admitted drug offenders in 2001 to 38% in 2011.

The number and proportion of parole violation admissions for drug offenders of all racial groups or Hispanic origin decreased between 2001 and 2011 (table 9), with an estimated 11,400 fewer readmissions of blacks (down 30%), 5,400 fewer whites (down 25%), and 5,200 fewer Hispanics (down 36%) in 2011. The number of parole violations by drug offenders other than possession among blacks decreased 92% (down 10,500).

TABLE 9
Estimated parole violation admissions to state prison, by race, Hispanic origin, and most serious offense, 1991, 2001, 2006, and 2011

Most serious offense[c]	1991[a]		2001[b]			2006[b]			2011[b]		
	White	Black	White[d]	Black[d]	Hispanic	White[d]	Black[d]	Hispanic	White[d]	Black[d]	Hispanic
Total	100%	100%	100%	100%	100%	100%	100%	100%	100%	100%	100%
Violent	20.6%	25.0%	20.9%	24.2%	25.6%	21.1%	25.2%	25.9%	22.8%	30.0%	30.2%
Murder[e]	1.4	1.7	0.8	1.5	1.3	0.6	1.4	1.0	0.7	1.4	1.2
Negligent manslaughter	0.6	0.4	0.3	0.2	0.3	0.5	0.3	0.3	0.4	0.2	0.3
Rape/sexual assault	5.0	2.7	4.5	2.8	2.8	4.6	3.4	3.4	5.5	4.4	3.9
Robbery	7.4	14.3	5.1	11.2	8.7	4.2	10.1	6.4	4.8	11.9	8.1
Assault	5.2	5.3	8.2	7.0	10.3	8.8	8.0	12.3	9.3	9.9	14.1
Other violent	0.9	0.5	2.0	1.5	2.2	2.3	1.9	2.5	2.1	2.2	2.7
Property	49.1%	36.6%	40.2%	27.4%	28.8%	39.9%	27.2%	31.3%	39.3%	25.9%	29.7%
Burglary	22.5	17.6	15.0	11.0	11.2	14.3	10.8	10.5	14.9	11.8	11.1
Larceny	13.1	11.0	10.2	9.0	7.8	8.3	7.7	6.1	7.8	6.3	5.7
Motor vehicle theft	5.3	3.5	5.4	2.7	5.3	6.4	3.0	8.5	5.8	2.6	7.3
Fraud	6.3	3.2	4.9	2.4	1.5	5.6	3.2	2.4	4.9	2.2	1.9
Other property	1.9	1.3	4.8	2.4	3.0	5.3	2.6	3.7	5.9	3.0	3.8
Drug	17.5%	33.2%	29.0%	42.0%	36.0%	26.9%	39.3%	30.2%	23.4%	31.4%	24.6%
Possession	7.0	8.4	12.9	8.0	8.7	12.3	7.9	10.9	10.2	7.5	10.0
Other drug[f]	10.6	24.7	16.1	34.0	27.3	14.6	31.4	19.3	13.2	23.9	14.6
Public order[g]	9.2%	3.5%	9.3%	6.0%	9.0%	11.5%	7.8%	12.3%	13.6%	11.9%	15.1%
Other/unspecified[h]	3.6%	1.8%	0.6%	0.4%	0.5%	0.6%	0.5%	0.4%	1.0%	0.9%	0.4%
Number of parole violation admissions	59,155	70,003	73,971	89,464	39,788	82,329	99,323	44,152	68,784	83,342	37,078

Note: Based on prisoners with a sentence of more than 1 year admitted to state prison on a conditional release violation, either for a release condition violation or for a new crime. Detail may not sum to total due to rounding, missing offense data, and racial categories not shown. Admission totals from National Prisoner Statistics Program. Offense distribution based on National Corrections Reporting Program administrative data. See *Methodology*. Estimates may vary from those previously published due to differences in methodology.

[a]Race data are weighted to represent the race/ethnicity distribution from the 1991 Survey of Inmates in State Correctional Facilities. See *Methodology*. The U.S. Office of Management and Budget published guidelines on the collection and reporting of Hispanic origin in 1997 (http://www.whitehouse.gov/omb/fedreg_1997standards/) and few states collected ethnicity data in 1991. Persons of Hispanic or Latino origin are included in the White and Black categories.

[b]Race and Hispanic origin data are weighted to represent the race/ethnicity distribution from the 2004 Survey of Inmates in State Correctional Facilities. See *Methodology*.

[c]Most serious offense refers to the original offense for which an inmate was sentenced, not the incident causing the parole revocation.

[d]Excludes persons of Hispanic or Latino origin and persons of two or more races.

[e]Includes nonnegligent manslaughter.

[f]Includes drug trafficking.

[g]Includes weapons, drunk driving, and court offenses; habitual offender sanctions; commercialized vice, morals, and decency offenses; and liquor law violations and other public order offenses.

[h]Includes juvenile offenses and other unspecified offense categories.

Sources: Bureau of Justice Statistics, National Prisoner Statistics Program and National Corrections Reporting Program, 1991, 2001, 2006, and 2011; and Survey of Inmates in State Correctional Facilities, 1991 and 2004.

Since 1991, the proportion of newly admitted violent offenders receiving prison sentences of less than 5 years has increased

The proportion of all new court commitments with sentences of less than 20 years was relatively stable across the 20-year period from 1991 to 2011—93% in 1991 and 2001, 92% in 2006, and 94% in 2011 (table 10). In 1991, 10% of all persons admitted on new convictions were sentenced to more than 1 year but less than 2 years in state prison. This increased to 14% in 2001, 2006, and 2011. The percentage of persons newly convicted for violent crimes and sentenced for less than 5 years increased from 37% in 1991 to 42% in 2001 and 44% in 2011. In 1991, 64% of offenders sentenced for drug offenses received less than 5 years, compared to 60% in 2001. In 2011, 69% of newly convicted violent offenders, 85% of drug offenders, and 88% of property offenders were sentenced to less than 10 years in prison.

In general, sentences for violent offenses were longer than for other types of crime. From 1991 to 2011, between 14% and 16% of prisoners admitted to state prison on new court commitments for violent offenses were sentenced to 20 years or more (including life or death sentences). A smaller proportion of violent offenders received sentences of life or death in 2011 (4.5%) than in 1991 (5.7%) or 2001 (4.9%), but the increased number of new court commitments for violent crimes in 2011 resulted in a greater number of convicted violent offenders with life or death sentences. Both the number (down 1,030) and percentage (down 84%) of inmates sentenced to life or death for drug offenses decreased between 1991 and 2011.

TABLE 10
Distribution of maximum sentence length for new court commitments to state prison, by most serious offense, 1991, 2001, 2006, and 2011

Most serious offense and maximum sentence length[a]	1991	2001	2006	2011
All new admissions	100%	100%	100%	100%
Less than 2 years[b]	9.9%	13.5%	13.7%	13.7%
2–4 years	48.1	45.2	43.8	43.5
5–9 years	23.8	24.3	22.2	24.4
10–19 years	11.4	9.9	12.1	12.3
20–49 years	4.5	3.7	3.6	4.1
50–99 years	0.2	0.4	0.4	0.4
100 years or more	0.0	1.4	2.8	0.1
Life/death[c]	2.1	1.6	1.4	1.5
Number of new court commitment admissions	317,237	365,229	442,111	398,709
Violent	100%	100%	100%	100%
Less than 2 years[b]	3.8%	6.8%	7.2%	7.4%
2–4 years	33.3	35.3	35.7	36.1
5–9 years	26.8	24.9	24.5	25.0
10–19 years	20.2	17.3	17.2	17.2
20–49 years	9.6	8.3	7.8	8.4
50–99 years	0.6	1.0	1.1	1.1
100 years or more	--	1.5	1.9	0.2
Life/death[c]	5.7	4.9	4.7	4.5
Number of new court commitment admissions	91,004	107,493	120,579	119,500
Property	100%	100%	100%	100%
Less than 2 years[b]	11.2%	15.6%	18.3%	18.8%
2–4 years	54.6	50.2	46.6	45.8
5–9 years	22.8	22.3	19.8	23.1
10–19 years	9.4	8.4	10.2	10.2
20–49 years	1.8	1.9	1.7	1.9
50–99 years	--	0.1	0.1	0.1
100 years or more	--	1.4	3.1	--
Life/death[c]	0.2	0.1	0.2	0.2
Number of new court commitment admissions	99,690	100,090	118,993	109,836

Continued on the next page

TABLE 10 (continued)
Distribution of maximum sentence length for new court commitments to state prison, by most serious offense, 1991, 2001, 2006, and 2011

Most serious offense and maximum sentence length[a]	1991	2001	2006	2011
Drug	100%	100%	100%	100%
Less than 2 years[b]	10.8%	12.7%	14.4%	15.1%
2–4 years	53.0	47.5	45.5	44.5
5–9 years	24.2	26.6	22.9	25.5
10–19 years	7.2	8.5	11.2	11.8
20–49 years	3.4	2.9	2.5	2.7
50–99 years	--	0.1	0.1	0.1
100 years or more	--	1.0	3.2	--
Life/death[c]	1.3	0.7	0.1	0.2
Number of new court commitment admissions	94,837	111,241	127,505	99,401
Public order[d]	100%	100%	100%	100%
Less than 2 years[b]	20.6%	18.0%	16.0%	15.1%
2–4 years	57.8	51.0	50.4	51.9
5–9 years	16.5	22.8	20.9	23.6
10–19 years	3.9	5.5	7.8	7.3
20–49 years	0.9	1.1	1.3	1.8
50–99 years	0.1	0.1	0.2	0.1
100 years or more	--	1.3	3.3	--
Life/death[c]	0.3	0.1	0.2	0.2
Number of new court commitment admissions	28,079	44,348	72,589	66,944
Other/unspecified[e]	100%	100%	100%	100%
Less than 2 years[b]	23.7%	10.0%	7.2%	7.1%
2–4 years	51.4	36.6	43.1	42.7
5–9 years	16.1	27.9	28.5	32.0
10–19 years	7.1	17.9	17.2	14.9
20–49 years	1.4	6.6	3.1	2.9
50–99 years	--	0.5	0.3	0.3
100 years or more	--	0.4	0.1	0.1
Life/death[c]	0.2	0.2	0.6	0.1
Number of new court commitment admissions	3,627	2,057	2,445	3,029

Note: Counts are based on state prisoners admitted on a new court commitment with a sentence of more than 1 year under the jurisdiction of state correctional officials. Detail may not sum to total due to rounding, missing offense and missing sentence length data. Admission totals from National Prisoner Statistics Program. Offense and sentence length distributions based on National Corrections Reporting Program administrative data. Analysis based on new court commitment admissions with known sentence lengths reported to NCRP. Estimates may vary from those previously published due to differences in methodology.

--Less than 0.05%.

[a]Maximum sentence length refers to the greatest amount of time an inmate is eligible to serve. It does not measure actual time served in prison.

[b]Includes prisoners sentenced to more than 1 year but less than 2 years.

[c]Includes prisoners sentenced to life, life without parole, life plus additional years, and death.

[d]Includes weapons, drunk driving, and court offenses; habitual offender sanctions; commercialized vice, morals, and decency offenses; and liquor law violations and other public order offenses.

[e]Includes juvenile offenses and other unspecified offense categories.

Sources: Bureau of Justice Statistics, National Prisoner Statistics Program and National Corrections Reporting Program, 1991, 2001, 2006, and 2011.

Violent offenders' longer sentences contribute to their increased proportion in the yearend prison population

The proportion of new court commitment and parole violation admissions for violent offenses is consistently smaller than the proportion of violent offenders in the prison population on December 31 of each year (table 11). This indicates that violent offenders are sentenced to, and are likely serving, relatively longer time in prison than inmates convicted of other types of crime.

TABLE 11
Estimated sentenced state prisoners on December 31, by most serious offense and type of admission, 1991, 2001, 2006, and 2011

Most serious offense[a]	1991		2001		2006		2011	
	New court commitment	Parole violation[a]	New court commitment	Parole violation[a]	New court commitment	Parole violation[a]	New court commitment	Parole violation[a]
Total	100%	100%	100%	100%	100%	100%	100%	100%
Violent	47.5%	26.8%	54.4%	35.4%	54.4%	36.0%	55.6%	39.6%
Murder[b]	12.2	2.8	13.6	4.7	13.1	4.8	13.5	6.0
Negligent manslaughter	2.3	0.8	1.6	0.5	1.6	0.5	1.6	0.5
Rape/sexual assault	9.0	3.1	12.7	5.2	13.3	6.2	13.3	6.0
Robbery	14.3	11.1	13.3	15.1	13.1	14.0	13.5	15.6
Assault	7.9	7.6	10.3	7.8	10.4	8.3	10.8	9.3
Other violent	1.8	1.5	2.9	2.0	2.9	2.0	2.9	2.2
Property	23.8%	34.6%	18.4%	29.9%	17.2%	29.0%	17.3%	27.3%
Burglary	10.8	14.1	9.4	14.4	8.5	14.3	9.2	14.5
Larceny	5.3	8.5	3.4	6.4	3.0	5.0	3.0	4.4
Motor vehicle theft	1.7	2.9	1.1	2.8	1.2	3.2	0.9	2.5
Fraud	3.6	6.0	2.3	3.2	2.4	3.5	2.1	2.8
Other property	2.3	3.2	2.3	3.1	2.2	2.9	2.1	3.0
Drug	22.0%	29.3%	19.8%	26.8%	18.4%	25.3%	15.8%	21.4%
Possession	7.4	13.2	4.3	6.1	4.7	7.2	3.7	6.0
Other drug[c]	14.5	16.1	15.5	20.7	13.7	18.1	12.0	15.4
Public order[d]	6.3%	8.9%	6.9%	7.4%	9.5%	9.1%	10.8%	10.8%
Other/unspecified[e]	0.5%	0.4%	0.5%	0.6%	0.5%	0.6%	0.5%	0.9%
Number of sentenced prisoners	626,694	106,222	980,728	218,573	1,065,662	254,988	1,131,210	200,966

Note: Based on prisoners with a sentence of more than 1 year admitted to state prison on a new court commitment or on a conditional release violation, either for a release condition violation or for a new crime. Detail may not sum to total due to rounding and missing offense data. Counts of sentenced prisoners admitted on new court commitments are based on the sentenced prisoner totals from the National Prisoner Statistics Program, and the ratio of new court commitments to parole violation admissions in the National Corrections Reporting Program yearend population. Offense distribution based on National Corrections Reporting Program administrative data. See *Methodology*. Estimates may vary from those previously published due to differences in methodology.

[a]For parole violation admissions, most serious offense refers to the original offense for which an inmate was sentenced, not the incident causing the parole revocation.
[b]Includes nonnegligent manslaughter.
[c]Includes drug trafficking.
[d]Includes weapons, drunk driving, and court offenses; habitual offender sanctions; commercialized vice, morals, and decency offenses; and liquor law violations and other public order offenses.
[e]Includes juvenile offenses and other unspecified offense categories.
Sources: Bureau of Justice Statistics, National Prisoner Statistics Program and National Corrections Reporting Program, 1991, 2001, 2006, and 2011.

From 1991 to 2011, violent offenses accounted for 27% to 30% of new court commitments with sentences of more than 1 year (figures 2 to 5). However, within the yearend populations for these years, inmates who were newly admitted for violent offenses represented 47% to 56% of the total state prison population. In contrast, property offenses made up 31% of new court commitments with sentences of more than 1 year in 1991, 27% in 2001 and 2006, and 28% in 2011, compared to between 17% and 24% of inmates originally admitted for property crimes in the prison population on December 31 of each year. Although these property offenders were sentenced to more than 1 year in prison, not all of them were serving a full year.

FIGURE 2

Violent offenders admitted to state prison and in the yearend prison population, by type of admission, 1991, 2001, 2006, and 2011

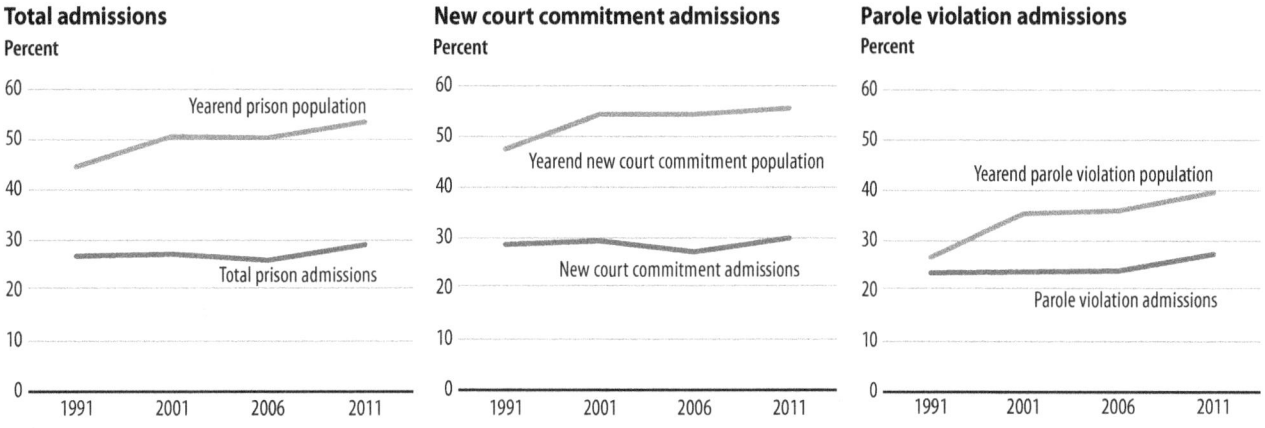

Note: Based on prisoners with a sentence of more than 1 year admitted to state prison on a new court commitment or conditional release violation.
Sources: Bureau of Justice Statistics, National Prisoner Statistics Program and National Corrections Reporting Program, 1991, 2001, 2006, and 2011.

FIGURE 3

Property offenders admitted to state prison and in the yearend prison population, by type of admission, 1991, 2001, 2006, and 2011

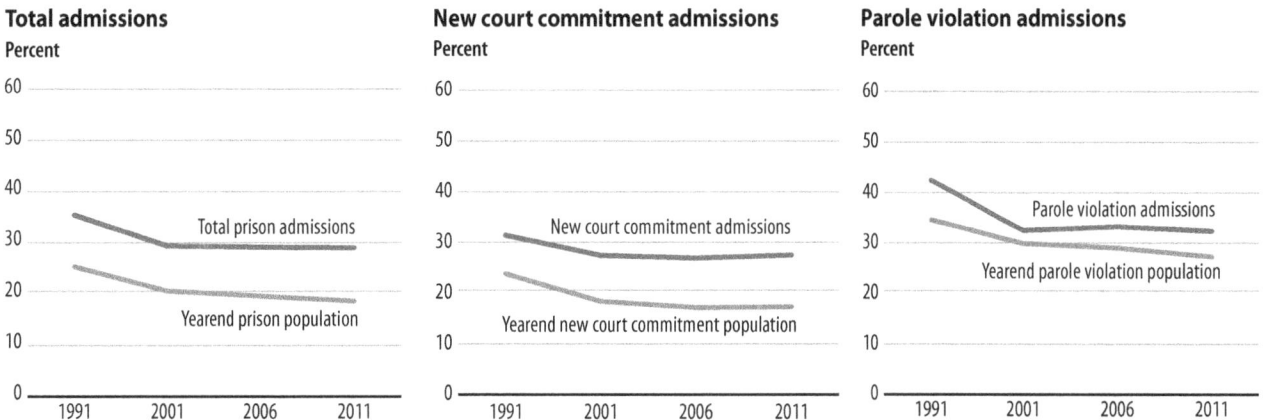

Note: Based on prisoners with a sentence of more than 1 year admitted to state prison on a new court commitment or conditional release violation.
Sources: Bureau of Justice Statistics, National Prisoner Statistics Program and National Corrections Reporting Program, 1991, 2001, 2006, and 2011.

Time served on parole violation admissions tends to be less than time served on new court commitments. This is reflected in the comparison of these admissions to the proportion of parole violators serving time on December 31 of the 4 years examined. The differences in the proportions of admissions and the yearend prison population were smaller than those observed for new court commitments across all offense categories, suggesting that inmates move through their confinement more quickly than offenders serving time on new court commitments for similar crimes. The only exception to this pattern occurred between 1991 and 2001 for admissions of public order and drug offense admissions of parole violators. In both cases, the proportion of parole violation admissions was less than that of parole violators in the yearend state prison population.

New admissions for violent offenses showed slight growth between 1991 and 2011, while the total share of violent offenders in the yearend prison population and among inmates readmitted on parole violations increased between 2001 and 2011.

FIGURE 4

Drug offenders admitted to state prison and in the yearend prison population, by type of admission, 1991, 2001, 2006, and 2011

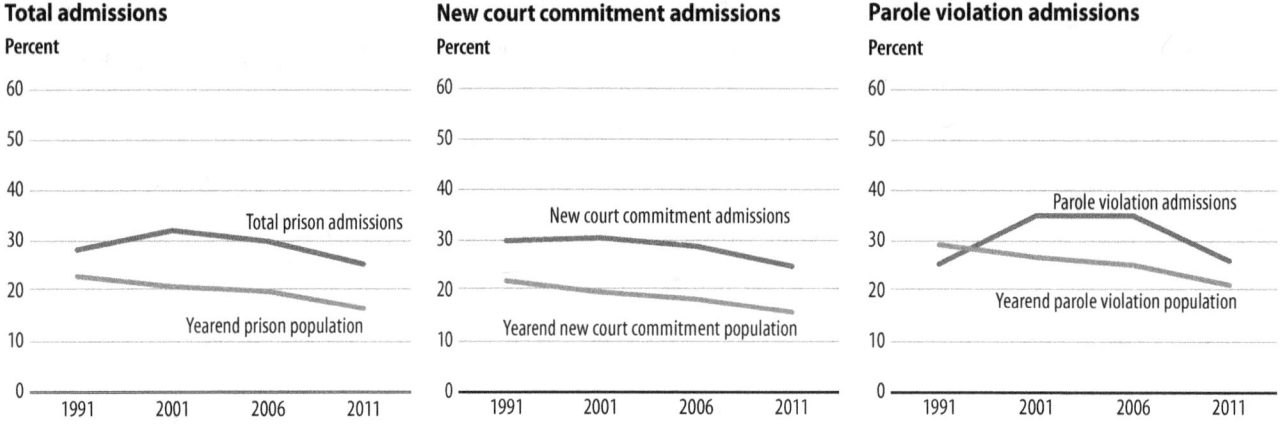

Note: Based on prisoners with a sentence of more than 1 year admitted to state prison on a new court commitment or conditional release violation.
Sources: Bureau of Justice Statistics, National Prisoner Statistics Program and National Corrections Reporting Program, 1991, 2001, 2006, and 2011.

FIGURE 5

Public order offenders admitted to state prison and in the yearend prison population, by type of admission, 1991, 2001, 2006, and 2011

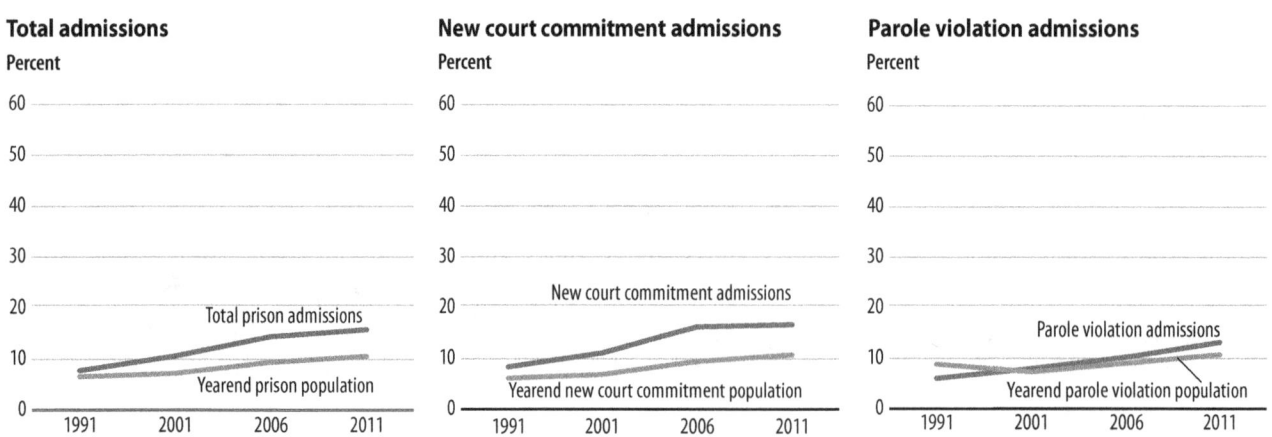

Note: Based on prisoners with a sentence of more than 1 year admitted to state prison on a new court commitment or conditional release violation.
Sources: Bureau of Justice Statistics, National Prisoner Statistics Program and National Corrections Reporting Program, 1991, 2001, 2006, and 2011.

State prisons released almost 24,900 more inmates than they admitted in 2011

State prisons admitted more offenders than they released in 1991, 2001, and 2006 (table 12). In 2011, there were about 24,900 more releases than admissions, and 59% of this difference was due to 14,600 more releases than admissions of drug offenders. Murder was the only offense for which admissions always outnumbered releases, while larceny had higher counts of releases except in 1991.

In 2011, conditional releases of violent offenders increased for inmates of all races and Hispanic origin, representing a quarter of whites and a third each of blacks and Hispanics released during 2011 (table 13). Black and Hispanic inmates convicted of violent crimes had the highest proportion of conditional releases across all offenses in 2011, in contrast to 2001 and 2006, when drug offenders were the most commonly released inmates among blacks and Hispanics. White inmates serving prison terms for property crimes had the highest number of conditional releases from 1991 to 2011, although this proportion declined over time concurrent with an increase in the number of releases of white violent and public order offenders.

TABLE 12
Estimated releases from state prison, by most serious offense, 1991, 2001, 2006, and 2011

Most serious offense	1991	2001	2006	2011
Total	100%	100%	100%	100%
Violent	24.1%	25.7%	25.0%	27.9%
Murder[a]	1.8	1.5	1.3	1.4
Negligent manslaughter	0.9	0.7	0.6	0.7
Rape/sexual assault	4.1	4.5	4.4	5.3
Robbery	10.4	8.7	7.2	7.8
Assault	6.0	8.3	9.3	10.3
Other violent	1.0	1.9	2.2	2.4
Property	37.5%	30.1%	30.0%	29.4%
Burglary	17.2	12.1	11.1	12.0
Larceny	10.3	7.7	6.9	6.1
Motor vehicle theft	2.7	2.8	3.5	3.1
Fraud	4.3	4.1	4.8	3.9
Other property	3.0	3.6	3.7	4.2
Drug	27.9%	33.7%	30.9%	26.7%
Possession	7.0	8.8	10.0	8.5
Other drug[b]	21.0	24.9	20.9	18.3
Public order[c]	8.6%	10.0%	13.5%	15.0%
Other/unspecified[d]	1.9%	0.5%	0.6%	1.0%
Number of releases	419,831	590,256	661,954	635,833

Note: Counts based on prisoners with a sentence of more than 1 year released from state prison. Excludes transfers, escapes, and those absent without leave (AWOL). Detail may not sum to total due to rounding and missing offense data. Release totals from National Prisoner Statistics Program. Offense distribution based on National Corrections Reporting Program administrative data. See *Methodology*. Estimates may vary from those previously published due to differences in methodology.
[a]Includes nonnegligent manslaughter.
[b]Includes drug trafficking.
[c]Includes weapons, drunk driving, and court offenses; habitual offender sanctions; commercialized vice, morals, and decency offenses; and liquor law violations and other public order offenses.
[d]Includes juvenile offenses and other unspecified offense categories.
Sources: Bureau of Justice Statistics, National Prisoner Statistics Program and National Corrections Reporting Program, 1991, 2001, 2006, and 2011.

TABLE 13
Estimated conditional releases from state prison, by race, Hispanic origin, and most serious offense, 1991, 2001, 2006, and 2011

Most serious offense[c]	1991[a]		2001[b]			2006[b]			2011[b]		
	White	Black	White[d]	Black[d]	Hispanic	White[d]	Black[d]	Hispanic	White[d]	Black[d]	Hispanic
Total	100%	100%	100%	100%	100%	100%	100%	100%	100%	100%	100%
Violent	20.6%	24.2%	22.1%	25.0%	26.3%	21.3%	26.3%	26.6%	25.5%	33.5%	33.1%
Murder[e]	1.3	1.5	0.9	1.8	1.4	0.7	1.6	1.2	1.0	2.0	1.6
Negligent manslaughter	1.0	0.6	0.7	0.4	0.4	0.7	0.4	0.5	0.9	0.6	0.6
Rape/sexual assault	5.5	2.4	5.6	2.6	3.9	4.9	2.9	3.8	6.3	4.0	5.3
Robbery	6.5	13.4	4.7	11.0	8.2	4.0	10.2	6.4	5.0	13.2	8.4
Assault	5.2	5.6	8.0	7.6	10.1	8.4	9.1	11.9	9.8	11.4	14.0
Other violent	1.1	0.7	2.3	1.6	2.3	2.4	2.1	2.8	2.5	2.4	3.2
Property	44.6%	32.5%	37.3%	25.6%	23.9%	35.8%	25.4%	28.0%	33.9%	23.0%	24.8%
Burglary	20.1	14.8	14.3	9.9	9.7	13.0	10.1	9.8	13.3	11.1	10.6
Larceny	11.6	9.8	9.0	7.8	6.0	7.7	6.8	5.3	7.0	5.2	4.6
Motor vehicle theft	3.6	2.4	3.9	2.2	4.2	4.5	2.3	7.2	3.6	1.8	4.6
Fraud	6.4	3.3	5.7	3.2	1.3	6.1	3.7	2.4	4.9	2.5	2.0
Other property	2.9	2.1	4.4	2.4	2.7	4.5	2.5	3.3	5.1	2.4	2.9
Drug	20.3%	37.4%	28.5%	42.1%	40.6%	28.7%	38.9%	32.5%	24.0%	30.1%	25.7%
Possession	6.5	10.1	11.4	8.7	9.0	11.8	9.5	11.5	9.5	8.6	10.2
Other drug[f]	13.8	27.2	17.2	33.4	31.5	17.0	29.3	21.0	14.5	21.5	15.5
Public order[g]	11.3%	4.4%	11.4%	6.9%	8.8%	13.5%	9.0%	12.4%	15.2%	12.3%	16.0%
Other/unspecified[h]	3.2%	1.5%	0.6%	0.4%	0.5%	0.7%	0.5%	0.5%	1.4%	1.1%	0.4%
Number of conditional releases	158,346	167,073	148,599	160,113	87,329	169,716	182,866	99,739	161,482	173,994	94,900

Note: Based on prisoners with a sentence of more than 1 year released from state prison to probation, supervised mandatory releases, and other unspecified conditional releases. Detail may not sum to total due to rounding, missing offense data, and racial categories not shown. Release totals from National Prisoner Statistics Program. Offense distribution based on National Corrections Reporting Program administrative data. Estimates may vary from those previously published due to differences in methodology.

[a]Race data are weighted to represent the race/ethnicity distribution from the 1991 Survey of Inmates in State Correctional Facilities. The U.S. Office of Management and Budget published guidelines on the collection and reporting of Hispanic origin in 1997 (http://www.whitehouse.gov/omb/fedreg_1997standards/) and few states collected ethnicity data in 1991. Persons of Hispanic or Latino origin are included in the White and Black categories. See *Methodology*.

[b]Race and Hispanic origin data are weighted to represent the race/ethnicity distribution from the 2004 Survey of Inmates in State Correctional Facilities. See *Methodology*.

[c]Most serious offense refers to the original offense for which an inmate was sentenced, not the incident causing the parole revocation.

[d]Excludes persons of Hispanic or Latino origin and persons of two or more races.

[e]Includes nonnegligent manslaughter.

[f]Includes drug trafficking.

[g]Includes weapons, drunk driving, and court offenses; habitual offender sanctions; commercialized vice, morals, and decency offenses; and liquor law violations and other public order offenses.

[h]Includes juvenile offenses and other unspecified offense categories.

Sources: Bureau of Justice Statistics, National Prisoner Statistics Program and National Corrections Reporting Program, 1991, 2001, 2006, and 2011; and Survey of Inmates in State Correctional Facilities, 1991 and 2004.

Admissions to California state prisons declined 65% from 2011 to 2012, while releases decreased 57%

During 2012, the first full year in which the California Public Safety Realignment (PSR) policy was implemented, both admissions to and releases from California state prisons decreased significantly. Between 2011 and 2012, total admissions to prisons in California declined 65%, from 96,700 admissions in 2011 to 34,300 in 2012 (table 14). The number of admissions in 2012 represented a 76% decrease from 2008, the year in which California admitted the most people to prison (140,800 admissions). (See *Prisoners in 2011*, NCJ 239808, BJS web, December 2012).

PSR was written to divert new admissions of nonviolent, nonserious, and nonsex offenders to local jail facilities starting on October 1, 2011.[1] Individuals convicted of serious, violent, or sex offenses continued to be admitted to state prison. In 2012, 48% of all admissions were for violent offenses (an increase from 31% in 2010 and 32% in 2011), and 14% of all admissions in 2012 were for drug offenses (a decrease from 25% in 2010). The proportion of admissions for property crimes declined by 10% over the period from 2010 to 2012, although admissions for public order offenses, which include weapons and habitual offender violations, increased in 2012.

---

[1]Offenses as specified in the Public Safety Realignment Act.

Continued on the next page

TABLE 14
California state prison admissions, by type of admission and most serious offense, 2010, 2011, and 2012

Most serious offense	2010			2011			2012		
	Total admissions	Parole violators[a]	New court commitments	Total admissions	Parole violators[a]	New court commitments	Total admissions	Parole violators[a]	New court commitments
Total	100%	100%	100%	100%	100%	100%	100%	100%	100%
Violent	30.8%	29.3%	33.3%	32.3%	29.2%	36.9%	48.1%	33.0%	52.6%
Murder[b]	1.8	0.8	3.6	2.2	0.8	4.2	4.9	2.0	5.8
Negligent manslaughter	0.5	0.3	0.7	0.5	0.3	0.7	0.9	0.3	1.0
Rape/sexual assault	5.6	6.1	4.8	5.4	5.3	5.5	5.9	1.8	7.1
Robbery	6.5	6.0	7.4	7.0	6.3	8.2	11.4	8.8	12.1
Assault	13.3	13.3	13.3	14.0	13.8	14.4	20.2	16.1	21.4
Other violent	3.0	2.7	3.6	3.2	2.7	3.9	4.9	4.0	5.1
Property	32.6%	34.2%	29.7%	31.8%	34.5%	27.6%	22.8%	28.0%	21.2%
Burglary	11.1	11.0	11.1	11.6	11.6	11.6	12.3	12.5	12.3
Larceny	7.9	8.2	7.3	7.1	7.9	5.9	3.5	5.3	3.0
Motor vehicle theft	7.0	8.4	4.3	6.6	8.3	4.1	3.2	5.6	2.5
Fraud	2.7	2.4	3.3	2.5	2.3	2.7	1.2	1.5	1.1
Other property	4.0	4.2	3.6	4.0	4.4	3.4	2.5	3.2	2.3
Drug offenses	24.7%	25.2%	23.9%	23.1%	24.0%	21.8%	13.5%	20.7%	11.3%
Possession	7.4	8.0	6.5	7.1	7.8	6.0	5.2	9.3	3.9
Trafficking	12.5	11.8	13.8	11.6	11.0	12.7	5.8	6.6	5.6
Other drug	4.8	5.4	3.6	4.4	5.1	3.2	2.5	4.7	1.9
Public order[c]	11.6%	11.0%	12.6%	12.5%	12.1%	13.2%	15.5%	18.1%	14.7%
Other/unspecified[d]	0.3%	0.3%	0.4%	0.3%	0.3%	0.4%	0.2%	0.2%	0.2%
Number of admissions	118,943	77,422	41,521	96,669	60,293	36,376	34,294	8,017	26,277

Note: Analysis based on National Corrections Reporting Program administrative data, which may vary slightly from National Prisoner Statistics Program data due to differences in data collection. Counts based on prisoners with a sentence of more than 1 year. Counts exclude transfers, escapes, and those absent without leave (AWOL). Totals include other conditional release violators, returns from appeal or bond, and other admissions. See *Methodology*.
[a]Includes all conditional release violators returned to prison for either violations of conditions of release or for new crimes.
[b]Includes nonnegligent manslaughter.
[c]Includes weapons, drunk driving, and court offenses; habitual offender sanctions; commercialized vice, morals, and decency offenses; and liquor law violations and other public order offenses.
[d]Includes juvenile offenses and other unspecified offense categories.
Source: Bureau of Justice Statistics, National Corrections Reporting Program, 2010, 2011, and 2012.

Between 2011 and 2012, the proportions of all admissions that were parole violations and new court commitments were reversed. In 2011, 62% of all admissions to California state prisons were parole violations, compared to 23% in 2012. New court commitments increased from 38% of all admissions in 2011 to 77% in 2012. In 2012, 33% of parole violation admissions to prisons and 53% of prisoners newly committed were violent offenders.

The number of inmates released from California prisons also declined in 2012, but at a slower rate than the decrease in admissions. In 2012, there were 47,500 releases from California prisons, 57% fewer than in 2011 when there were 109,500 releases (table 15). In 2012, 37% of all releases were of violent offenders, compared to 29% in 2010. Prisoners convicted of aggravated assault and robbery accounted for the majority of the increase in released prisoners. While violent offenders accounted for 29% of conditional releases in 2010, this proportion had increased to 67% in 2012.

Continued on the next page

TABLE 15
California state prison releases, by type of release and most serious offense, 2010, 2011, and 2012

Most serious offense	2010			2011			2012		
	Total releases	Unconditional releases[a]	Conditional releases[b]	Total releases	Unconditional releases[a]	Conditional releases[b]	Total releases	Unconditional releases[a]	Conditional releases[b]
Total	100%	100%	100%	100%	100%	100%	100%	100%	100%
Violent	29.0%	40.3%	28.7%	30.7%	16.7%	32.5%	36.9%	18.2%	66.8%
Murder[c]	1.2	2.3	1.1	1.4	0.3	1.4	2.4	0.2	5.4
Negligent manslaughter	0.5	0.6	0.5	0.5	0.3	0.5	0.6	0.3	1.1
Rape/sexual assault	5.3	9.3	5.2	5.4	2.4	5.8	5.2	1.3	11.3
Robbery	6.1	7.9	6.1	6.7	2.1	7.4	9.0	1.7	20.8
Assault	13.0	16.0	12.9	13.6	9.4	14.2	16.1	12.6	22.0
Other violent	2.9	4.1	2.9	3.1	2.1	3.2	3.6	2.0	6.2
Property	32.8%	24.6%	33.0%	32.4%	36.8%	31.8%	27.8%	33.3%	19.1%
Burglary	10.7	8.6	10.8	11.2	10.6	11.2	11.6	9.6	15.1
Larceny	8.0	6.0	8.0	7.7	9.3	7.5	5.7	8.5	1.1
Motor vehicle theft	7.1	4.6	7.2	6.9	8.3	6.7	5.2	7.8	1.1
Fraud	2.8	2.3	2.8	2.7	3.9	2.5	2.2	3.5	0.3
Other property	4.1	3.0	4.1	4.0	4.7	3.9	3.0	3.9	1.5
Drug	26.5%	23.0%	26.6%	24.8%	32.5%	23.7%	21.9%	32.6%	4.6%
Possession	7.6	7.5	7.6	7.0	9.2	6.8	5.1	7.6	0.9
Trafficking	13.7	10.3	13.8	13.3	17.7	12.7	13.9	20.6	3.2
Other drug	5.2	5.3	5.2	4.5	5.6	4.3	2.9	4.3	0.6
Public order[d]	11.4%	11.6%	11.5%	11.9%	13.8%	11.6%	13.2%	15.7%	9.2%
Other/unspecified[e]	0.3%	0.5%	0.3%	0.3%	0.3%	0.3%	0.3%	0.3%	0.2%
Number of releases	121,918	1,728	119,941	109,467	13,676	95,541	47,454	29,485	17,756

Note: Analysis based on National Corrections Reporting Program administrative data, which may vary slightly from National Prisoner Statistics Program data due to differences in data collection. Counts based on prisoners with a sentence of more than 1 year. Counts exclude transfers, escapes, and those absent without leave (AWOL). Totals include deaths, releases to appeal or bond, and other releases. See *Methodology*.
[a]Includes expirations of sentence, communtations, and other unconditional releases.
[b]Includes releases to probation, supervised mandatory releases, and other unspecified conditional releases.
[c]Includes nonnegligent manslaughter.
[d]Includes weapons, drunk driving, and court offenses; habitual offender sanctions; commercialized vice, morals, and decency offenses; and liquor law violations and other public order offenses.
[e]Includes juvenile offenses and other unspecified offense categories.
Source: Bureau of Justice Statistics, National Corrections Reporting Program, 2010, 2011, and 2012.

Similar to the pattern of admission types, unconditional releases accounted for less than 2% of total releases in 2010 and 12% in 2011, compared to 62% in 2012. In 2012, 37% of prisoners were released with post custody conditions, down from 98% in 2010. Drug and property offenses accounted for 33% each of all unconditional releases in 2012. While the percentage of violent offenders unconditionally released from California state prisons decreased from 40% in 2010 to 18% in 2012, the increase in the total number of unconditional releases in 2012 resulted in a net increase of violent offenders with this type of prison release, from 670 offenders in 2010 to 5,400 offenders in 2012.

Released prisoners in California are returned to the county in which they were originally sentenced. While this does not guarantee that a former prisoner will continue to live in the same county, it provides a proxy measure to identify the counties most immediately influenced by state prison releases. In 2012, 30% of all inmates released from California state prisons (14,800 persons) were returned to Los Angeles County, followed by San Bernardino (4,400

inmates or 9.1% of all releases) and San Diego counties (3,500 or 7.3% of all releases) (table 16). Almost two-thirds of inmates released from prison to these three counties had no conditions placed on their release. Only four counties (Alameda, Colusa, Inyo, and Trinity) received more conditional releases from state prison than inmates released unconditionally.

While Los Angeles County received the largest number of inmates released from state prisons in 2012, when compared to the general population of each county, Los Angeles had a prison release rate of 14.9 per 10,000 county residents. Eighteen counties with smaller general populations had higher rates of prison release in their communities. Kings County (population 150,800) received 507 prison releases, but had a rate of 33.6 releases per 10,000 residents. After Kings County, Yuba (29.0 releases per 10,000 residents), Tehama (28.8 releases per 10,000 residents), and Shasta (24.4 releases per 10,000 residents) counties had the highest rates of released prisoners.

TABLE 16
California state prison releases, by type of release and county of sentencing, 2012

County[c]	All releases		Unconditional releases[a]		Conditional releases[b]		County general population	
	Count	Percent of total state releases	Count	Percent of total county releases	Count	Percent of total county releases	Total, July 1, 2012[d]	Release rate per 10,000 residents[e]
Total	48,621	100%	29,920	~	18,346	~	37,826,160	12.9
Alameda	1,117	2.3%	488	43.7%	622	55.7%	1,540,790	7.2
Alpine	0	0.0	0	/	0	/	1,127	/
Amador	65	0.1	53	81.5	12	18.5	36,899	17.6
Butte	438	0.9	299	68.3	133	30.4	221,118	19.8
Calaveras	53	0.1	35	66.0	18	34.0	45,045	11.8
Colusa	31	0.1	13	41.9	18	58.1	21,614	14.3
Contra Costa	462	1.0	232	50.2	227	49.1	1,069,803	4.3
Del Norte	38	0.1	22	57.9	15	39.5	28,359	13.4
El Dorado	136	0.3	80	58.8	53	39.0	180,599	7.5
Fresno	1,739	3.6	1,117	64.2	613	35.3	946,823	18.4
Glenn	41	0.1	23	56.1	16	39.0	28,208	14.5
Humboldt	229	0.5	155	67.7	73	31.9	134,923	17.0
Imperial	144	0.3	92	63.9	51	35.4	178,659	8.1
Inyo	18	0.0	6	33.3	11	61.1	18,637	9.7
Kern	1,889	3.9	1,322	70.0	560	29.6	855,522	22.1
Kings	507	1.0	337	66.5	169	33.3	150,843	33.6
Lake	127	0.3	77	60.6	47	37.0	64,394	19.7
Lassen	33	0.1	27	81.8	6	18.2	33,650	9.8
Los Angeles	14,817	30.5	9,300	62.8	5,398	36.4	9,911,665	14.9
Madera	210	0.4	136	64.8	74	35.2	151,790	13.8
Marin	85	0.2	47	55.3	36	42.4	254,882	3.3
Mariposa	20	0.0	15	75.0	5	25.0	17,817	11.2
Mendocino	97	0.2	53	54.6	44	45.4	88,566	11.0
Merced	302	0.6	172	57.0	130	43.0	261,708	11.5
Modoc	7	0.0	4	57.1	3	42.9	9,518	7.4
Mono	4	0.0	2	50.0	2	50.0	14,258	2.8
Monterey	522	1.1	292	55.9	228	43.7	422,868	12.3
Napa	142	0.3	72	50.7	70	49.3	138,577	10.2
Nevada	47	0.1	30	63.8	16	34.0	98,202	4.8
Orange	2,870	5.9	1,701	59.3	1,152	40.1	3,071,933	9.3

Continued on the next page

TABLE 16 (continued)
California state prison releases, by type of release and county of sentencing, 2012

County[c]	All releases		Unconditional releases[a]		Conditional releases[b]		County general population	
	Count	Percent of total state releases	Count	Percent of total county releases	Count	Percent of total county releases	Total, July 1, 2012[d]	Release rate per 10,000 residents[e]
Placer	285	0.6	191	67.0	92	32.3	360,680	7.9
Plumas	25	0.1	16	64.0	9	36.0	19,523	12.8
Riverside	2,942	6.1	1,828	62.1	1,087	36.9	2,244,399	13.1
Sacramento	1,887	3.9	1,089	57.7	778	41.2	1,439,874	13.1
San Benito	61	0.1	38	62.3	23	37.7	56,527	10.8
San Bernardino	4,402	9.1	2,785	63.3	1,594	36.2	2,065,016	21.3
San Diego	3,528	7.3	2,182	61.8	1,318	37.4	3,147,220	11.2
San Francisco	474	1.0	260	54.9	207	43.7	820,349	5.8
San Joaquin	1,076	2.2	618	57.4	452	42.0	699,003	15.4
San Luis Obispo	254	0.5	148	58.3	104	40.9	271,021	9.4
San Mateo	519	1.1	305	58.8	213	41.0	736,362	7.0
Santa Barbara	548	1.1	335	61.1	212	38.7	427,358	12.8
Santa Clara	1,536	3.2	825	53.7	691	45.0	1,828,597	8.4
Santa Cruz	144	0.3	77	53.5	67	46.5	267,569	5.4
Shasta	436	0.9	310	71.1	121	27.8	178,477	24.4
Sierra	7	0.0	4	57.1	3	42.9	3,089	22.7
Siskiyou	76	0.2	46	60.5	27	35.5	44,598	17.0
Solano	502	1.0	327	65.1	175	34.9	415,913	12.1
Sonoma	369	0.8	220	59.6	146	39.6	489,283	7.5
Stanislaus	870	1.8	589	67.7	277	31.8	522,651	16.6
Sutter	174	0.4	102	58.6	72	41.4	95,351	18.2
Tehama	183	0.4	136	74.3	46	25.1	63,623	28.8
Trinity	8	0.0	2	25.0	5	62.5	13,470	5.9
Tulare	746	1.5	437	58.6	303	40.6	451,627	16.5
Tuolumne	77	0.2	43	55.8	32	41.6	54,339	14.2
Ventura	692	1.4	399	57.7	288	41.6	834,109	8.3
Yolo	398	0.8	281	70.6	115	28.9	204,314	19.5
Yuba	212	0.4	125	59.0	87	41.0	73,021	29.0

Note: Counts based on prisoners with a sentence of more than 1 year. Counts exclude transfers, escapes, and those absent without leave (AWOL). Totals include deaths, releases to appeal or bond, and other releases. See *Methodology*. Analysis based on National Corrections Reporting Program administrative data, which may vary slightly from National Prisoner Statistics Program data due to differences in data collection and missing data.

~ Not applicable.

/ Not calculated.

[a]County in which inmate was originally sentenced. In California, inmates are released to the county in which they were sentenced.

[b]Includes expirations of sentence, communtations, and other unconditional releases.

[c]Includes releases to probation, supervised mandatory releases, and other unspecified conditional releases.

[d]Preliminary county population counts for July 1, 2012 obtained from State of California, Department of Finance, E-2. California County Population Estimates and Components of Change by Year—July 1, 2010–2012, December 2012.

[e]Prison release rate per 10,000 California county residents of all ages.

Source: Bureau of Justice Statistics, National Corrections Reporting Program, 2010, 2011, and 2012, and Department of Finance, State of California.

The 2012 yearend U.S. sentenced prison population declined 1.8%, driven by a decrease in the number of state prisoners

A total of 27,400 fewer prisoners were sentenced to more than 1 year in state and federal prisons at yearend 2012, than at yearend 2011, a decrease of almost 2% (table 17). The federal prison system had the largest sentenced prison population (196,600 prisoners) of any jurisdiction in 2012, followed by Texas (157,900 inmates), California (134,200 inmates), Florida (101,900 inmates), and New York (54,100 inmates). With the federal population, these five jurisdictions accounted for 43% of the sentenced U.S. prison population in 2012. Texas, California, and Florida accounted for 30% of the sentenced state prison population in 2012.

California (down 10%) had the largest percentage decrease in prison population, followed by Arkansas (down 9%), Wisconsin and Colorado (down 7% each). The prison populations in New Hampshire (up 7%) and North Dakota (up 6%) led the 24 jurisdictions with sentenced population increases in 2012. Females comprised almost 7% of the state prison population and 6% of the federal system in 2012.

TABLE 17
Sentenced state and federal prisoners, by sex, December 31, 2011 and 2012

Jurisdiction	2011			2012			Percent change, 2011–2012		
	Total	Males	Females	Total	Males	Females	Total	Males	Females
U.S. Total	1,538,847	1,435,141	103,706	1,511,480	1,410,191	101,289	-1.8%	-1.7%	-2.3%
Federal[a]	197,050	184,901	12,149	196,574	184,258	12,316	-0.2%	-0.3%	1.4%
State	1,341,797	1,250,240	91,557	1,314,906	1,225,933	88,973	-2.0%	-1.9%	-2.8%
Alabama	31,271	28,823	2,448	31,437	28,915	2,522	0.5	0.3	3.0
Alaska[b]	2,894	2,616	278	2,974	2,690	284	2.8	2.8	2.2
Arizona	38,370	35,098	3,272	38,402	35,065	3,337	0.1	-0.1	2.0
Arkansas	16,037	14,938	1,099	14,615	13,567	1,048	-8.9	-9.2	-4.6
California	149,025	140,972	8,053	134,211	128,180	6,031	-9.9	-9.1	-25.1
Colorado	21,978	19,957	2,021	20,462	18,739	1,723	-6.9	-6.1	-14.7
Connecticut[b]	12,549	11,865	684	11,961	11,314	647	-4.7	-4.6	-5.4
Delaware[b]	4,003	3,815	188	4,129	3,913	216	3.1	2.6	14.9
Florida	103,055	95,913	7,142	101,930	94,945	6,985	-1.1	-1.0	-2.2
Georgia	53,955	50,211	3,744	53,990	50,510	3,480	0.1	0.6	-7.1
Hawaii[b]	3,910	3,527	383	3,819	3,439	380	-2.3	-2.5	-0.8
Idaho	7,739	6,854	885	7,985	6,977	1,008	3.2	1.8	13.9
Illinois[c]	48,427	45,562	2,865	49,348	46,599	2,749	1.9	2.3	-4.0
Indiana	28,890	26,391	2,499	28,822	26,256	2,566	-0.2	-0.5	2.7
Iowa[d]	9,057	8,336	721	8,686	7,917	769	-4.1	-5.0	6.7
Kansas[d]	9,327	8,647	680	9,398	8,724	674	0.8	0.9	-0.9
Kentucky	20,952	18,575	2,377	21,466	18,919	2,547	2.5	1.9	7.2
Louisiana	39,709	37,325	2,384	40,170	37,781	2,389	1.2	1.2	0.2
Maine	1,952	1,810	142	1,932	1,797	135	-1.0	-0.7	-4.9
Maryland	22,252	21,301	951	21,281	20,410	871	-4.4	-4.2	-8.4
Massachusetts	10,316	9,822	494	9,999	9,567	432	-3.1	-2.6	-12.6
Michigan	42,904	40,995	1,909	43,594	41,605	1,989	1.6	1.5	4.2
Minnesota	9,800	9,156	644	9,938	9,228	710	1.4	0.8	10.2
Mississippi	20,585	19,115	1,470	21,426	19,884	1,542	4.1	4.0	4.9
Missouri	30,829	28,254	2,575	31,244	28,541	2,703	1.3	1.0	5.0
Montana	3,678	3,274	404	3,609	3,210	399	-1.9	-2.0	-1.2
Nebraska	4,511	4,159	352	4,594	4,255	339	1.8	2.3	-3.7
Nevada[c]	12,639	11,672	967	12,744	11,706	1,038	0.8	0.3	7.3
New Hampshire	2,614	2,444	170	2,790	2,583	207	6.7	5.7	21.8
New Jersey	23,834	22,762	1,072	23,225	22,164	1,061	-2.6	-2.6	-1.0
New Mexico	6,855	6,230	625	6,574	5,954	620	-4.1	-4.4	-0.8
New York	55,262	52,973	2,289	54,073	51,846	2,227	-2.2	-2.1	-2.7
North Carolina	35,102	33,030	2,072	34,983	32,846	2,137	-0.3	-0.6	3.1
North Dakota	1,423	1,276	147	1,512	1,341	171	6.3	5.1	16.3
Ohio	50,964	47,061	3,903	50,876	47,008	3,868	-0.2	-0.1	-0.9
Oklahoma	24,024	21,693	2,331	24,830	22,369	2,461	3.4	3.1	5.6
Oregon	14,459	13,343	1,116	14,801	13,574	1,227	2.4	1.7	9.9
Pennsylvania	51,390	48,657	2,733	50,918	48,219	2,699	-0.9	-0.9	-1.2
Rhode Island[b]	2,065	1,984	81	1,999	1,916	83	-3.2	-3.4	2.5
South Carolina	22,233	20,940	1,293	21,725	20,485	1,240	-2.3	-2.2	-4.1

Continued on the next page

TABLE 17 (Continued)
Sentenced state and federal prisoners, by sex, December 31, 2011 and 2012

Jurisdiction	2011			2012			Percent change, 2011–2012		
	Total	Males	Females	Total	Males	Females	Total	Males	Females
South Dakota	3,530	3,092	438	3,644	3,221	423	3.2	4.2	-3.4
Tennessee	28,479	26,070	2,409	28,411	26,048	2,363	-0.2	-0.1	-1.9
Texas	163,552	151,343	12,209	157,900	146,292	11,608	-3.5	-3.3	-4.9
Utah	6,877	6,264	613	6,960	6,321	639	1.2	0.9	4.2
Vermont[b]	1,598	1,496	102	1,516	1,443	73	-5.1	-3.5	-28.4
Virginia	38,130	35,321	2,809	37,044	34,150	2,894	-2.8	-3.3	3.0
Washington	17,808	16,420	1,388	17,254	15,920	1,334	-3.1	-3.0	-3.9
West Virginia	6,803	6,056	747	7,027	6,235	792	3.3	3.0	6.0
Wisconsin	21,998	20,858	1,140	20,474	19,379	1,095	-6.9	-7.1	-3.9
Wyoming	2,183	1,944	239	2,204	1,966	238	1.0	1.1	-0.4

Note: Jurisdiction refers to the legal authority of state or federal correctional officials over a prisoner, regardless of where the prisoner is held. Counts are based on prisoners with sentences of more than 1 year under the jurisdiction of state or federal correctional officials. As of December 31, 2001, sentenced felons from the District of Columbia are the responsibility of the Federal Bureau of Prisons.

[a]Includes inmates held in nonsecure privately operated community corrections facilities and juveniles held in contract facilities.

[b]Prisons and jails form one integrated system. Data include total jail and prison populations.

[c]State did not submit 2012 National Prisoner Statistics (NPS) Program data, so population estimates for 2012 are imputed. See *Methodology* for discussion of imputation strategy.

[d]Change in reporting methods. See *National Prisoner Statistics Program jurisdiction notes*.

Source: Bureau of Justice Statistics, National Prisoner Statistics Program, 2011–2012.

Imprisonment rates continued to decline for most race, ethnicity, sex, and age groups

Compared to age-, sex-, and race-specific imprisonment rates in 2011, rates in 2012 remained the same or decreased for all but Hispanic males ages 60 to 64, which increased from 685 per 100,000 U.S. residents to 687 per 100,000 residents (table 18) (see *Prisoners in 2011*, NCJ 239808, BJS web, December 2012).

Male and female white prisoners of all age groups had lower imprisonment rates than male and female black and Hispanic prisoners. Overall, black males were 6 times and Hispanic males 2.5 times more likely to be imprisoned than white males in 2012. Hispanic males ages 18 to 19 were more than 3 times as likely as white males of the same age to be imprisoned, while all other age groups were at least twice as likely as white males to be serving a prison sentence. Black males had imprisonment rates at least 4 times those of white males in all age groups. The rates for black males age 39 or younger were more than 6 times greater than white males of the same age. Male inmates ages 18 to 19 had the largest imprisonment rate disparity between whites and blacks. Black males in this age group were almost 9.5 times more likely than white males to be in prison.

Almost 1% of all male residents in the United States were imprisoned at yearend 2012. A total of 2.8% of black, 0.5% of white, and 1.2% of Hispanic males were in state or federal prison on December 31, 2012. Among black males, this represents a decline from the rate in 2011 (3%). Between 4% and 7% of black males ages 20 to 49 were prison inmates. Black males ages 30 to 34 had the highest incarceration rate (6,932 prisoners per 100,000 black male U.S. residents ages 30 to 34). This age group also had the highest imprisonment rates among white and Hispanic males in 2012.

Among female prisoners in 2012, black females ages 18 to 19 were 3 times more likely to be imprisoned than white females. Hispanic females in this age group had imprisonment rates nearly twice those of white females. White and Hispanic females approached parity imprisonment rates among prisoners ages 35 to 44. Hispanic females age 65 or older were more than twice as likely as white females of this age to be serving time in prison, the age group of greatest disparity. Black and white female imprisonment rates were closest among prisoners ages 25 to 39, when black females were less than twice as likely as white females to be imprisoned.

TABLE 18
Imprisonment rate of sentenced state and federal prisoners per 100,000 U.S. residents, by sex, race, Hispanic origin, and age, December 31, 2012

| Age group | Total[a] | Males | | | | | Females | | | | |
		All male[a]	White[b]	Black[b]	Hispanic	Other[a,b]	All female[a]	White[b]	Black[b]	Hispanic	Other[a,b]
Total[c]	480	909	463	2,841	1,158	972	63	49	115	64	90
18–19	228	428	148	1,393	485	417	18	11	35	22	14
20–24	805	1,476	654	4,284	1,726	1,480	100	78	163	101	141
25–29	1,113	2,032	998	6,138	2,412	2,245	166	138	263	165	242
30–34	1,198	2,213	1,098	6,932	2,594	2,304	175	147	287	163	237
35–39	1,060	1,975	992	6,258	2,338	2,042	149	128	251	130	165
40–44	902	1,682	927	5,148	1,986	1,623	130	108	230	113	148
45–49	772	1,451	814	4,433	1,731	1,458	107	82	204	97	130
50–54	539	1,031	581	3,219	1,352	1,144	65	49	128	66	100
55–59	326	636	360	2,016	983	689	34	24	71	42	52
60–64	193	386	238	1,144	687	456	16	12	32	22	16
65 or older	66	146	99	423	280	193	4	3	6	7	8

Note: Counts based on prisoners with sentences of more than 1 year under the jurisdiction of state or federal correctional officials. Imprisonment rate is the number of prisoners under state or federal jurisdiction with a sentence of more than 1 year per 100,000 U.S. residents of corresponding sex, age, and race/ethnicity. Resident population estimates are from the U.S. Census Bureau for January 1 of the following year. Illinois and Nevada did not submit 2012 data to the National Prisoner Statistics Program, so their jurisdiction counts are imputed. See *Methodology*.
[a]Includes American Indians, Alaska Natives, Asians, Native Hawaiians, other Pacific Islanders, and persons identifying two or more races.
[b]Excludes persons of Hispanic or Latino orgin.
[c]Includes persons age 17 or younger.
Sources: Bureau of Justice Statistics, National Prisoner Statistics Program, 2012; Federal Justice Statistics Program, 2012; National Corrections Reporting Program, 2011; and Survey of Inmates in State and Local Correctional Facilities, 2004.

Other select findings

- In 2012, the number of prisoners released increased in 27 states (appendix table 1).

- Blacks accounted for 40% of all unconditional releases from state prison in 2001, 2006, and 2011 (appendix table 2).

- Inmates under age 45 accounted for 80% of federal and state prison admissions in 2012, compared to 72% of the yearend prison population in 2012, and 77% of released prisoners (appendix tables 3–5).

- The total U.S. prison population declined for the third consecutive year in 2012, to 1,570,400 prisoners on December 31, 2012 (appendix table 6).

- The proportion of the U.S. prison population housed in private prisons increased from 8.2% in 2011 to 8.7% in 2012 (appendix table 7).

- A total of 137,200 inmates were in the custody of private prisons at yearend 2012, a 5% increase over the 131,000 inmates in 2011.

- The number of prison inmates housed in local jail facilities on December 31, 2012 (83,600 inmates) was 2% higher than at yearend 2011.

- In 2012, the number of inmates held in local jails increased in 16 states.

- Four states housed more than 25% of their prison populations in local jails on December 31, 2012: Louisiana (52%), Kentucky (38%), Tennessee (30%), and Mississippi (29%).

- U.S. prisons held 9,900 fewer persons identified as noncitizens in 2012, compared to 102,800 noncitizen inmates in 2011 (appendix table 8). Because state and federal departments of corrections have varying definitions of noncitizen, readers should exercise caution when interpreting these results.

- State prisons held 1,300 inmates under age 18 in custody on December 31, 2012.

- Based on their reported custody counts, 18 states and the BOP were operating prison systems above 100% of their maximum reported facility capacity (appendix table 9).

- The number of prisoners serving a sentence for violent offenses in federal prison in 2012 (11,700 inmates) decreased 21% from 2011 (14,900 inmates) (appendix table 10).

- Drug offenders accounted for 50% of the male federal prison population and 58% of the female federal prison population in 2012 (appendix table 11).

- On December 31, 2012, 12% of prisoners in the federal prison system were serving time for immigration offenses and 15% had been convicted of weapons offenses.

National Prisoner Statistics Program jurisdiction notes

Alabama—Prisons have not recently been rated for official capacity, but the majority of Alabama prisons are operating in a state of overcrowding. Currently, there are 26,339 beds in operation; this represents the physical capacity for inmates but is not based on staffing, programs, and services. Operational capacity differs from the BJS definition.

Alaska—Prisons and jails form one integrated system. All NPS data include jail and prison populations housed in state and out of state. Jurisdictional totals include individuals in electronic and special monitoring programs who are under the jurisdiction of the state of Alaska. All capacity measures are the same as in 2011. The count of Asian inmates includes Pacific Islanders. Alaska does not report type of admission or release. Total admissions and releases include Alaskan reported values, but state and national totals by type of admission and release do not.

Arizona—Jurisdiction counts are based on custody data and inmates in contracted beds. The "other admissions" category includes four males and one female who were mistakenly released and readmitted during 2012.

Arkansas—Jurisdiction counts of prisoners held in local jails include county jail back-up and inmates participating in the Act 309 Program, which provides additional space for the care and custody of state inmates on a temporary basis in state-certified adult detention facilities operated by counties and cities.

California—Population counts for inmates with maximum sentences of more than 1 year include felons who are temporarily absent, such as in court, in jail, or in a hospital. The majority of temporarily absent inmates are absent for fewer than 30 days. Population counts for unsentenced inmates include civil addicts who are enrolled for treatment and are not serving a criminal conviction sentence, but are under the jurisdiction of the California Department of Corrections and Rehabilitation. In addition, the counts of unsentenced inmates include persons housed in out-of-state contract facilities. California is unable to differentiate between inmates held in federal facilities and those held in other states' facilities. Changes in design capacity are based on information from an annual facilities planning and management report.

Colorado—Population counts include a small, undetermined number of inmates with a maximum sentence of 1 year or less. Admission and release data for inmates who are absent without leave (AWOL) or who have escaped are estimated. Design and operational capacities do not include the privately run facilities in Colorado.

Connecticut—Prisons and jails form one integrated system. All NPS data include jail and prison populations. New court commitment admissions include inmates admitted in 2012 on accused status, but who received a sentence later in 2012. Legislation in July 1995 abolished the capacity law. A facility's capacity is a fluid number based on the needs of the department. The needs are dictated by security issues, populations, court decrees, legal mandates, staffing, and physical plant areas of facilities that are serving other purposes or have been decommissioned. The actual capacity of a facility is subject to change.

Delaware—Prisons and jails form one integrated system. All NPS data include jail and prison populations. Capacity counts include the halfway houses under the Department of Corrections.

Federal Bureau of Prisons (BOP)—Data reflect inmates under BOP jurisdiction on December 30, 2012. Jurisdiction counts include inmates housed in secure private facilities where the BOP had a direct contract with a private operator, as well as inmates housed in secure facilities where there was a subcontract with a private provider at a local government facility. Jurisdiction counts also include inmates housed in jail or short-term detention and others held in state-operated or other nonfederal secure facilities. Counts include 8,932 inmates (7,798 males and 1,134 females) held in nonsecure, privately operated community corrections centers/halfway houses and 2,659 offenders on home confinement (2,278 males and 381 females). A total of 99 male and 6 female juveniles were held in contract facilities; these inmates were included in the jurisdiction totals but excluded from the counts of private, locally operated, or federally operated facilities. Due to information system configuration, Asians and Native Hawaiians or other Pacific Islanders are combined, and inmates of Hispanic origin are included in the race categories. On December 30, 2012, BOP held 71,714 male and 4,378 female inmates of Hispanic origin. Other admissions include hospitalization and treatment. Parole violation counts combine those with and without a new sentence. Expirations of sentence include good-conduct releases that usually have a separate and distinct term of supervision, as well as releases from the residential drug abuse treatment program. Other releases include vacated sentences, completion of hospitalization or treatment, and court-ordered terminations. The BOP population on December 30, 2012, was 176,658 inmates (excluding contracted and private facilities), and the rated capacity on that date was 128,615. The crowding rate was 37%.

Florida—Other conditional releases include provisional release supervision, conditional medical release, program supervision, and parole reinstatement.

Georgia—Females are not housed in privately operated correctional facilities in Georgia. Subtotals of race, sex, and sentence length for jurisdiction and custody counts were adjusted by the Georgia Department of Corrections using interpolation to match the overall totals.

Hawaii—Prisons and jails form one integrated system. All NPS data include jail and prison populations. In custody and jurisdiction counts, sentenced felon probationers and probation violators are included with the counts of prisoners with a total maximum sentence of 1 year or less. Jurisdiction counts include dual-jurisdiction (state of Hawaii or federal) inmates currently housed in federal facilities and in contracted beds. Hawaii does not have a rated capacity for the integrated prisons and jail system. Information on foreign nationals held in correctional facilities was based on self-reports by inmates.

Idaho—Idaho defines rated capacity as 100% of maximum capacity and operational capacity as 95% of maximum capacity. Design capacity is based on original facility-designed occupancy.

Illinois—Illinois did not submit NPS data in 2012. See Methodology for a description of the data imputation procedure.

Iowa—In 2009, the Iowa Department of Corrections began including offenders on work release, the Operating While Intoxicated population, and Iowa inmates housed in out-of-state prisons and in jurisdiction counts. Iowa data included in BJS reports prior to 2009 were custody counts only. Jurisdiction counts include Iowa offenders housed in prisons in other jurisdictions who are under Iowa's jurisdiction. The data quality and collection methodology were updated in 2012; therefore, changes from previous years' counts may reflect these updates. Absent without leave (AWOL) admissions and releases are for the work release and the Operating While Intoxicated population. Escape admissions and releases are for the prison population only; this differs from the 2011 counts, which included escapes from work release.

Kansas—Jurisdiction counts of inmates with sentences of less than 1 year are available for 2012, but not for 2011. Admissions and releases reflect movements of the custody population with the exception of transfers, which include all Kansas prisoners regardless of custody status.

Kentucky—The decrease in the number of unconditional releases between 2011 and 2012 is due to the implementation of a mandatory reentry supervision law, which became effective on January 1, 2012.

Louisiana—Jurisdiction and capacity counts are correct as of December 27, 2012.

Maine—Fewer male state prisoners are housed in county facilities due to overcrowding at the local level. The state has been adding capacity and double-bunking at prisons.

Maryland—The number of inmates with maximum sentences of more than 1 year is estimated by taking the percentages for these prisoners from the automated totals and applying them to the manual totals submitted for NPS. The number of male inmates included in the jurisdiction count of prisoners held in other state facilities may include a small number of female inmates. Maryland's system does not capture Hispanic origin. An undetermined number of Native Hawaiians and other Pacific Islanders may be included in the count of American Indian/Alaska Natives. Maryland's system does not distinguish between AWOL and escape releases, nor does it record the sex of inmates housed in out-of-state private prisons. The count of admissions by new court commitments may include a small but undetermined number of returns from appeal or bond. The count of unconditional releases includes court-ordered releases and a small but undetermined number of releases to appeal or bond. Other release types include interstate compact releases and releases of new admissions that were counted twice.

Massachusetts—By law, offenders in Massachusetts may be sentenced to terms of up to 2.5 years in locally operated jails and correctional institutions. This population is excluded from the state count, but is included in published population counts and rates for local jails and correctional institutions. Jurisdiction counts exclude approximately 3,271 inmates in the county system (local jails and houses of correction) who are serving a sentence of more than 1 year, but these inmates are included in imprisonment rate calculations at the request of the Massachusetts Department of Corrections. Jurisdiction and custody counts may include a small but undetermined number of inmates who were remanded to court; transferred to the custody of another state, federal, or locally operated system; or subsequently released. Due to the opening of a new correctional facility for females, the admissions, releases, and custody population of county-sentenced females serving under the jurisdiction of the Department of Corrections has decreased. After legislative changes to reduce discretionary parole releases in 2011 that caused fluctuations in the number and rate of persons released on parole, these measures remained stable during 2012. This has resulted in an apparently higher parole rate in 2012 than in 2011 for both males and females. In 2012, 261 inmates received unconditional court releases due to falsification of drug tests by one of the chemists in the state drug lab.

Michigan—Operational capacity includes institution and camp net operating capacities, as well as the population of community programs on December 31, 2012. Michigan's new database system treats Hispanic as an ethnicity rather than a race. Because this is currently an optional field, the numbers for Hispanics are significantly underreported, and the state included them in the white race category. Escape releases and admissions consist predominantly of zero-tolerance escapes from community residential programs.

Minnesota—Jurisdiction counts include inmates temporarily housed in local jails, on work release, or on community work crew programs. Minnesota only measures operational capacity.

Admissions and releases due to AWOL or escape, returns from or releases to appeal or bond, and releases due to transfer are not included in Minnesota's database file.

Mississippi—Custody counts exclude county regional facilities, while jurisdiction counts include these facilities. Local jails and county regional facilities are included in the jurisdiction count of inmates housed at local facilities. Parole and conditional release violators are not distinguished by their sentence status in the Mississippi file.

Missouri—The Missouri Department of Corrections does not have the design capacity of its older prisons, nor does it update design capacity for prison extension or improvements. Missouri does not use a rated capacity. The state defines operational capacity as the number of available beds, including those temporarily offline. Noncitizen data are based on self-reported place of birth.

Nebraska—By statute, inmates are housed where they are sentenced by the judge and are never housed in local jails or by another state to ease prison crowding. Nebraska defines operational capacity as its stress capacity, which is 125% of design capacity for designated facilities. The total design and operational capacity for institutions that house females includes only one multicustody facility. The department operates two co-ed facilities that represent a design capacity of 290, and that are counted in the male design and operational capacities.

Nevada—Nevada did not submit NPS data in 2012. See *Methodology* for a description of the data imputation procedure.

New Hampshire—The new offender database management system reports the number of inmates who are under New Hampshire's jurisdiction but housed in other state facilities in a different manner from NPS submissions prior to 2010. New Hampshire's operating capacity is defined as the inmate population on any given day.

New Jersey—Population counts for inmates with a maximum sentence of more than 1 year include inmates with sentences of 1 year. The New Jersey Department of Corrections has no jurisdiction over inmates with sentences of less than 1 year or over unsentenced inmates. Reporting of other conditional release admissions has changed from 2011 to better reflect the sentence status of inmates. Other releases include inmates brought too soon from the county jails into the state prison system, then released back to the county jails. New Jersey has recently undertaken a review of its prison system capacity, resulting in updated counts in 2012.

New Mexico—New Mexico does not include its inmates housed in other states under the interstate compact agreement in its total jurisdiction count. According to BJS definitions, these inmates should be included in the total state jurisdiction, and were in this report.

North Carolina—As of December 1, 2011, North Carolina prisons no longer house misdemeanor offenders with sentences of less than 180 days. Rated capacity is not available. Captured escapees are not considered a prison admission type in North Carolina, and escape is not considered a type of prison release. Supervised mandatory releases are postrelease offenders. Postrelease supervision is defined as a reintegration program for serious offenders who have served extensive prison terms. This form of supervision was created by the Structured Sentencing Act of 1993.

North Dakota—Capacities include a new facility that opened in 1998 and account for double bunking in the state penitentiary.

Ohio—Population counts for inmates with a maximum sentence of more than 1 year include an undetermined number of inmates with a sentence of 1 year or less. Counts of inmates who are under Ohio's jurisdiction but housed in federal or other state facilities are estimates. Counts of admission and release types reflect revised reporting methods. Admissions of parole violators without a new sentence include only formally revoked violators. Returns and conditional releases involving transitional control inmates are reported only after movement from confinement to a terminal release status occurs.

Oklahoma—Jurisdiction counts exclude inmates from other states who were serving time in Oklahoma prisons under the interstate compact and inmates sentenced to the Department of Corrections but not yet in custody. Jurisdiction counts include offenders in a Department of Corrections jail program, those in court, and escapees in the custody of local jails. Most inmates with sentences of less than 1 year were part of the Oklahoma Delayed Sentencing Program for Young Adults. Offenders in the custody of other states and the BOP are mostly escapees. Capacity counts have changed in Oklahoma, as only Department of Corrections facilities have an approved capacity determined by the Board of Corrections according to the standards of the American Correctional Association. Noncitizen status is determined by country of birth.

Oregon—Most offenders with a maximum sentence of less than 1 year remain under the custody of local counties rather than the Oregon Department of Corrections. Oregon does not recognize rated capacity.

Pennsylvania—All Pennsylvania inmates housed in Virginia were brought back to serve time in Pennsylvania in March 2012.

Rhode Island—Prisons and jails form one integrated system. All NPS data include jail and prison populations. Jurisdiction counts include inmates who have dual jurisdiction, or those serving Rhode Island sentences out of state while serving that state's sentence as well. The Rhode Island data system records Hispanic as a race rather than an ethnicity and does not capture Native Hawaiian/Other Pacific Islanders or persons identifying as two or more races. Prison admissions classified as escape returns include admissions under home confinement, serving out of state, and minimum-security facilities.

South Carolina—The December 31, 2012, custody count of unsentenced individuals includes Interstate Compact Commission inmates. As of July 1, 2003, the South Carolina Department of Corrections (SCDC) began releasing inmates due for release and housed in SCDC institutions on the first day of each month. Since January 1, 2013, was a holiday, inmates eligible for release on January 1 were released on December 31, 2012. Therefore, the inmate count was at its lowest point for the month on December 31, 2012. All inmates in private facilities in South Carolina were housed in private medical facilities. Conditional release counts include inmates released under community supervision after serving 85% of their sentence under truth in sentencing. The SCDC has implemented new intensive supervision services, which are designed to promote community safety and ensure the successful reentry of young offenders back into the community. South Carolina uses the operational capacity concept in its management reports and other requested surveys.

South Dakota—Custody and jurisdiction counts of inmates serving a maximum sentence of 1 year or less included those under the sentence of probation who, as a condition of probation, must serve up to 180 days in state prison. The custody count of unsentenced inmates included all holds for the U.S. Marshals Service (sentenced and unsentenced). Commutations are not tracked separately in the South Dakota reporting system; however, they are included in expiration of sentence, supervised mandatory release, or other conditional releases. South Dakota does not separate discretionary and presumptive parole releases. The operational capacity reported is planned capacity. South Dakota does not have rated or design capacities.

Tennessee—The sex of six inmates could not be identified and were counted as males in the jurisdiction counts. Eleven inmates could not be assigned to a race category, including five females and the six assigned male inmates.

Texas—Offenders in custody were all offenders serving time in a facility owned and operated by the Texas Department of Criminal Justice at the time of data collection. Jurisdiction counts include offenders in custody and those held in privately operated prisons, intermediate-sanction facilities, substance abuse felony punishment facilities, pre-parole transfer facilities, and halfway houses; offenders temporarily released to a county for less than 30 days; and offenders awaiting paperwork for transfer to state-funded custody. Capacities exclude county jail beds because they do not have a minimum or maximum number of beds available for paper-ready and bench-warrant inmates. Admissions and releases include offenders received into an intermediate-sanction facility, which is a sanction in lieu of revocation. These offenders were counted in the parole violator category.

Vermont—Prisons and jails form one integrated system. All NPS data include jail and prison populations. Hispanic origin and persons identifying as two or more races are not collected or recorded in Vermont.

Virginia—Jurisdiction counts were for December 31, 2012. As of September 1, 1998, the state is responsible for inmates with a sentence of 1 year or more, or a sentence of 12 months plus 1 day. The state was responsible for a 1-year sentence, while local authorities were responsible for a 12-month sentence. Inmates with a sentence of 12 months or less were not the responsibility of the state. New court commitments are based on fiscal year 2012, while parole violation admissions and all releases are based on calendar year 2012. The Virginia Department of Corrections maintains a count of beds (called authorized capacity) that is provided as the measure of rated capacity in this survey. The number of beds assigned by rating officials (Virginia Department of Corrections) to institutions takes into account the number of inmates who can be accommodated based on staff, programs, services, and design. Native Hawaiians and Pacific Islanders are included in the Asian race category.

Washington—Offenders sentenced to 1 year or less and unsentenced offenders generally reside in county jails, but revisions to law allow certain inmates with sentences of less than 1 year to be housed in prison. These inmates are included in the total jurisdiction counts. Native Hawaiians and Pacific Islanders are included in the Asian race category.

Wisconsin—Custody and jurisdiction counts include 722 temporary probation and parole placements. The jurisdiction count excludes 27 male and 2 female prisoners because they were not serving a Wisconsin sentence. In 2012, both the female custody and jurisdiction populations increased, probably due to more new court commitments and parole violation admissions. Wisconsin does not code escapes as releases and returns from the escape as admissions. In 2012, 19 males and 1 female were on escape status. Design capacities for local jails and for federal, other state, and private facilities are excluded from the total design capacity measure. The reported design capacity includes the following facilities currently housing Wisconsin adult inmates: a state juvenile facility with a design capacity of 400, a non-Department of Corrections facility with a design capacity of 362, and 29 beds contracted in 20 Wisconsin county jails to temporarily house Department of Corrections inmates. The number of contracted beds has declined substantially from the 97 beds reported in 2011.

Terms and definitions

Adult imprisonment rate—The number of prisoners under state or federal jurisdiction sentenced to more than 1 year per 100,000 U.S. residents age 18 or older.

Average annual change—Average (mean) annual change across a specific period.

Capacity, design—The number of inmates that planners or architects intended for a facility.

Capacity, highest—The maximum number of beds reported across the three capacity measures: design capacity, operational capacity, and rated capacity.

Capacity, lowest—The minimum number of beds across the three capacity measures: design capacity, operational capacity, and rated capacity.

Capacity, operational—The number of inmates that can be accommodated based on a facility's staff, existing programs, and services.

Capacity, rated—The number of beds or inmates assigned by a rating official to institutions within a jurisdiction.

Conditional releases—Includes discretionary parole, mandatory parole, postcustody probation, and other unspecified conditional releases.

Conditional release violators—Readmission to prison of persons released to discretionary parole, mandatory parole, postcustody probation, and other unspecified conditional releases.

Custody—Prisoners held in the physical custody of state or federal prisons or local jails, regardless of sentence length or authority having jurisdiction.

Imprisonment rate—The number of prisoners under state or federal jurisdiction sentenced to more than 1 year per 100,000 U.S. residents of all ages.

Inmate—A person incarcerated in a local jail, state prison, federal prison, or a private facility under contract to federal, state, or local authorities.

Jail—A confinement facility usually administered by a local law enforcement agency that is intended for adults, but sometimes holds juveniles, for confinement before and after adjudication. Such facilities include jails and city or county correctional centers; special jail facilities, such as medical treatment or release centers; halfway houses; work farms; and temporary holding or lockup facilities that are part of the jail's combined function. Inmates sentenced to jail facilities usually have a sentence of 1 year or less. Alaska, Connecticut, Delaware, Hawaii, Rhode Island, and Vermont operate integrated systems, which combine prisons and jails.

Jurisdiction—The legal authority of state or federal correctional officials over a prisoner, regardless of where the prisoner is held.

New court commitments—Admissions into prison of offenders convicted and sentenced by a court, usually to a term of more than 1 year, including probation violators and persons with a split sentence to incarceration followed by court-ordered probation or parole.

Parole violators—All conditional release violators returned to prison for either violating conditions of release or for new crimes.

Prison—A long-term confinement facility, run by a state or the federal government, that typically holds felons and offenders with sentences of more than 1 year. However, sentence length may vary by state. Alaska, Connecticut, Delaware, Hawaii, Rhode Island, and Vermont operate integrated systems, which combine prisons and jails.

Prisoner—An individual confined in a correctional facility under the legal authority (jurisdiction) of state or federal correctional officials.

Sentenced prisoner—A prisoner sentenced to more than 1 year.

Supervised mandatory releases—Conditional release with postcustody supervision generally occurring in jurisdictions using determinate sentencing statutes.

Unconditional releases—Expirations of sentences, commutations, and other unspecified unconditional releases.

Methodology

Started in 1926 under a mandate from Congress, the National Prisoner Statistics (NPS) Program collects annual data on prisoners at yearend. The Bureau of Justice Statistics (BJS) sponsors the survey, and the U.S. Census Bureau serves as the data collection agent. BJS depends entirely on voluntary participation by state departments of corrections and the Federal Bureau of Prisons (BOP) for NPS data.

The NPS distinguishes between inmates in custody and prisoners under jurisdiction. To have custody of a prisoner, a state or the BOP must hold that inmate in one of its facilities. To have jurisdiction over a prisoner, the state or BOP must have legal authority over that prisoner, regardless of where the prisoner is incarcerated or supervised. Some states were unable to provide counts that distinguish between custody and jurisdiction. (See *National Prisoner Statistics Program jurisdiction notes* to determine which states did not distinguish between custody and jurisdiction counts.)

The NPS jurisdiction counts include persons held in prisons, penitentiaries, correctional facilities, halfway houses, boot camps, farms, training or treatment centers, and hospitals. Counts also include prisoners who were temporarily absent (less than 30 days), in court, or on work release; housed in privately operated facilities, local jails, or other state or federal facilities; and serving concurrent sentences for more than one correctional authority.

The NPS custody counts include all inmates held within a respondent's facilities, including inmates housed for other correctional facilities. The custody counts exclude inmates held in local jails and in other jurisdictions. With a few exceptions, the NPS custody counts include inmates held in privately operated facilities.

Respondents to NPS surveys are permitted to update prior counts of prisoners held in custody and under jurisdiction. Some statistics on jurisdiction and sentenced prison populations for prior years have been updated in this report. All tables showing data based on jurisdiction counts, including tables of imprisonment rates, were based on the updated and most recently available data that respondents provided.

Admissions include new court commitments, parole violator returns, and other conditional release violator returns; transfers from other jurisdictions; returns of prisoners who were absent without leave (AWOL), with or without a new sentence; escape returns, with or without a new sentence; returns from appeal or bond, and other admissions. For reporting purposes, BJS admission counts exclude transfers from other jurisdictions, AWOL returns, and escape returns.

Releases include unconditional releases (e.g., expirations of sentence or commutations), conditional releases (e.g., probations, supervised mandatory releases, or discretionary paroles), deaths, AWOLs, escapes from confinement, transfers to other jurisdictions, releases to appeal or bond, and other releases. For reporting purposes, BJS release counts exclude AWOLs, escapes, and transfers to other jurisdictions.

The NPS has historically included counts of inmates in the combined jail/prison systems in Alaska, Connecticut, Delaware, Hawaii, Rhode Island, and Vermont. The District of Columbia has not operated a prison system since yearend 2001. Felons sentenced under the District of Columbia criminal code are housed in federal facilities. Jail inmates in the District of Columbia are included in the Annual Survey of Jails. Some previously published prisoner counts and the percentage change in population include jail inmates in the District of Columbia for 2001, the last year of collection.

Additional information about the NPS, including the data collection instrument, is available on the BJS website at www.bjs.gov.

Nonreporting states

As of September 13, 2013, Illinois and Nevada had not reported any 2012 custody, jurisdiction, admission, release, or capacity data to the NPS. For both states, BJS compared past NPS submissions with analogous counts reported on their departments of corrections websites. If the ratio of past NPS data to the website data from the same year was stable over 6 years, BJS assumed that the website data could be used in this report. To generate estimates for Nevada, BJS used statistical data published on the Nevada Department of Corrections website (http://www.doc.nv.gov/sites/doc/files/pdf/stats/2012/12/StatFacts122012.pdf) for total and sex-specific custody, jurisdiction, admission and release counts, and a race and Hispanic origin distribution of the custody population as of December 31, 2012. BJS applied the 2011 proportion of unsentenced prisoners and prisoners with sentences of 1 year or less or more than 1 year to the 2012 custody and jurisdiction totals, which assumes that the distribution of sentence length did not change between 2011 and 2012. BJS also assumed that the proportion of the Nevada prison jurisdiction population housed in local jails in 2012 was the same as that reported in 2011. Similarly, BJS used the 2011 distribution of admission and release types to generate estimates from the 2012 admission and release totals. BJS used an estimate of operating capacity from June 30, 2012 (http://www.doc.nv.gov/sites/doc/files/pdf/stats/2012/12/SS_QRII_FY13.pdf). Estimates of the custody counts for Nevada were compared with the state's submission of National Corrections Reporting Program (NCRP) data.

November 30, 2012, is the date closest to December 31, 2012, for which data were available on the Illinois Department of Corrections website (http://www2.illinois.gov/idoc/reportsandstatistics/Documents/IDOC_Quarterly%20Report_Jan_%202013.pdf). Illinois has reported identical custody and jurisdiction data to the NPS for the past 10 years; therefore, BJS made the assumption that the 2012 custody and jurisdiction counts would again be the same. BJS applied the 2011 distribution of sentence length (unsentenced, sentenced to 1 year or less, sentenced to more than 1 year) to the 2012 counts. The 2011 race and Hispanic origin distribution from Illinois was applied to the custody and jurisdiction total count from November 30, 2012.

The 2011 distribution of admission and release types was used to estimate the types of admissions and releases in 2012. BJS obtained monthly counts of admissions and releases from two quarterly reports (http://www2.illinois.gov/idoc/reportsandstatistics/Documents/IDOC_Quarterly%20Report_Apr_%202013.pdf and http://www2.illinois.gov/idoc/reportsandstatistics/Documents/IDOC_Quarterly%20Report_Jul%202012.pdf). Since these were not sex-specific counts, after summing to obtain 2012 totals, BJS applied the 2011 sex ratios for admissions and releases to the 2012 data, assuming that the proportion of males and females entering or exiting prison had not changed during 2012. Finally, BJS applied the 2011 sex-specific admission and release type distributions on the 2012 totals. Capacity counts were obtained from the April 2013 Illinois Department of Corrections quarterly report, and reflect state prison capacity as of February 28, 2013.

The imputed counts were used to calculate overall state and national totals of prisoners, and are footnoted in state-specific tables.

Estimating yearend counts of prison population, admissions, and releases by age, sex, and race or Hispanic origin

National-level estimates of the number of persons by race admitted to, released from, or under the jurisdiction of state prisons on December 31, 2012, were based on an adjustment of NPS counts to comply with Office of Management and Budget (OMB) definitions of race and Hispanic origin. OMB defines persons of Hispanic or Latino origin as a separate category. Race categories are defined exclusive of Hispanic origin. OMB adopted guidelines for the collection of these data in 1997, requiring the collection of data on Hispanic origin in addition to data on race.

Not all NPS providers' information systems categorize race and Hispanic origin in this way; in 1991, the earliest time point in the analysis, only a few states were able to report information on Hispanics separately from race. BJS adjusts the NPS data on race and Hispanic origin by the ratio of the relative distribution of prisoners by race and Hispanic origin in self-report inmate surveys that use OMB categories for race to the relative distribution of prisoners by race and Hispanic origin in the NPS data. This ratio was calculated for the year(s) in which BJS had an inmate survey and NPS data. For this report, the 1991 Survey of Inmates in State Correctional Facilities was used to calculate the ratio used for statistics on racial distributions in 1991; however, because so few states reported Hispanic origin in the 1991 NPS, BJS did not estimate statistics for Hispanics in 1991. The 2004 Survey of Inmates in State Correctional Facilities was used for the 2001, 2006, 2011, and 2012 time points. The ratio obtained by comparing the within-year relative distributions by race and Hispanic origin was then multiplied by the NPS distribution in a year to generate the estimate of persons by race and Hispanic origin.

Estimates of the total number of sentenced prisoners, admissions, and releases by age, sex, race, and Hispanic origin on December 31, 2012, were generated by creating separate totals for federal and state prisons. For the federal estimates, each sex-race count that BOP reported to the NPS was multiplied by the ratio of the age category count within the sex-race combination in the Federal Justice Statistics Program (FJSP) to the FJSP total count within the sex-race combination (e.g., FJSP white males ages 18 to 19 divided by FJSP white males). The resulting product yielded the FJSP-adjusted NPS counts for each sex-race combination by age group (e.g., white male prisoners ages 18 to 19 in the federal prison system). State prison age distributions for the NPS use a similar sex-race ratio adjustment based on individual-level data from the NCRP. State and federal estimates were added together to obtain national estimates for prison admissions, prison releases, and yearend prison populations.

Estimating imprisonment rates by age, sex, and race or Hispanic origin

Age-specific imprisonment rates for each age-sex-race group were calculated by dividing the estimated number of sentenced prisoners within each age group under jurisdiction on December 31, 2012, by the estimated number of U.S. residents in each age group on January 1, 2013. The result was multiplied by 100,000 and rounded to the nearest whole number. Totals by sex include all prisoners and U.S. residents, regardless of race or Hispanic origin.

Estimating offense distribution in the state prison population, admissions, and releases by age, sex, and race or Hispanic origin

Total counts of admissions and releases excluded transfers, escapees, and those absent without leave (AWOL). Parole violation admissions included all conditional release violators returned to prison for either violations of conditions or for new crimes. BJS employed a ratio adjustment method to weight the individual-level race and Hispanic origin or sex-specific offense data from the NCRP to the state prison control totals for sex and the estimated race or Hispanic origin from the NPS, thereby yielding a national offense distribution for state prisoners. Inmates missing offense data were excluded from the analysis prior to the weighting. Because data submission for the NCRP typically lags behind that of the NPS, offense distribution estimates are published for the previous calendar year.

Prison capacities

State and federal correctional authorities provide three measures of their facilities' capacity: design capacity, operational capacity, and rated capacity. Estimates of the prison populations as a percentage of capacity are based on a state or federal custody population. In general, state capacity and custody counts exclude inmates held in private facilities, although five states include prisoners held in private facilities as part of the capacity of their prison systems: Florida, Georgia, Idaho, Louisiana, and Mississippi. For these states, prison population as a percentage of capacity includes private facilities.

Admissions and releases of sentenced prisoners by jurisdiction, 2011 and 2012

Jurisdiction	Admissions during—[a]					Releases during—[b]				
	2011 Total	2012 Total	Percent change, 2011–2012	2012 New court commitments[c]	2012 Parole violations[c,d]	2011 Total	2012 Total	Percent change, 2011–2012	2012 Unconditional[c,e]	2012 Conditional[c,f]
U.S. Total	671,551	609,781	-9.2%	444,591	152,780	691,072	637,411	-7.8%	213,204	408,186
Federal	60,634	55,938	-7.7	51,241	4,696	55,239	56,037	1.4	55,079	591
State	610,917	553,843	-9.3	393,350	148,084	635,833	581,374	-8.6	158,125	407,595
Alabama	11,387	11,203	-1.6	9,201	1,116	11,052	11,253	1.8	3,740	7,358
Alaska[c,g,h]	3,789	3,906	3.1	/	/	3,599	3,774	4.9	/	/
Arizona	13,030	12,970	-0.5	10,469	2,394	13,149	13,000	-1.1	2,119	10,146
Arkansas	7,059	5,782	-18.1	4,588	1,182	7,252	6,298	-13.2	313	5,940
California	96,669	34,294	-64.5	26,277	8,017	109,467	47,454	-56.6	29,485	17,756
Colorado	9,455	9,409	-0.5	5,009	4,396	9,367	10,919	16.6	1,315	9,426
Connecticut[g]	5,881	5,659	-3.8	4,711	800	6,379	6,014	-5.7	3,355	2,634
Delaware[g]	3,031	3,017	-0.5	2,610	389	3,600	4,012	11.4	304	3,651
Florida	33,399	32,265	-3.4	31,129	119	34,673	33,661	-2.9	21,426	11,879
Georgia	14,877	15,743	5.8	13,940	1,794	15,309	14,021	-8.4	4,510	9,388
Hawaii[g]	1,366	1,524	11.6	854	670	1,404	1,631	16.2	315	654
Idaho	3,531	4,568	29.4	4,306	262	4,079	4,617	13.2	958	3,644
Illinois[i]	31,167	30,877	-0.9	19,881	10,807	31,155	30,108	-3.4	5,602	24,381
Indiana	18,389	18,694	1.7	15,377	3,014	18,422	18,555	0.7	1,888	16,608
Iowa	4,709	4,877	3.6	3,754	1,114	5,105	5,221	2.3	1,330	3,810
Kansas	4,954	5,060	2.1	3,701	1,300	4,671	4,795	2.7	1,159	3,614
Kentucky	15,479	15,399	-0.5	11,262	4,137	14,571	16,215	11.3	3,272	12,852
Louisiana	16,161	17,325	7.2	12,197	5,104	16,580	17,104	3.2	1,511	15,419
Maine	921	846	-8.1	563	283	1,049	1,108	5.6	703	405
Maryland	9,811	9,396	-4.2	5,859	3,534	9,829	10,347	5.3	1,308	8,974
Massachusetts[j]	2,856	2,635	-7.7	2,385	250	2,484	2,871	15.6	2,266	574
Michigan	13,165	13,888	5.5	7,477	4,100	14,374	13,199	-8.2	961	9,972
Minnesota	7,214	7,412	2.7	4,735	2,677	7,734	7,730	-0.1	1,049	6,666
Mississippi	8,410	8,559	1.8	6,412	2,108	8,197	7,725	-5.8	1,370	6,239
Missouri	17,979	18,216	1.3	9,748	8,465	17,823	17,957	0.8	1,625	16,238
Montana	2,063	2,020	-2.1	1,519	501	2,101	2,089	-0.6	284	1,789
Nebraska	2,410	2,761	14.6	2,162	459	2,391	2,688	12.4	722	1,950
Nevada[i]	5,545	5,336	-3.8	4,335	930	5,910	5,399	-8.6	1,989	3,374
New Hampshire	1,616	1,696	5.0	868	813	1,881	1,555	-17.3	98	1,440
New Jersey	10,110	9,976	-1.3	7,504	2,472	11,485	10,817	-5.8	6,040	4,618
New Mexico	3,491	3,580	2.5	2,225	1,355	3,529	3,371	-4.5	1,034	2,322
New York	23,257	23,065	-0.8	13,853	9,158	24,460	24,224	-1.0	2,696	21,261
North Carolina	11,523	12,098	5.0	11,469	629	11,878	12,327	3.8	8,119	4,132
North Dakota	950	1,160	22.1	640	520	1,013	1,069	5.5	188	874
Ohio	22,150	21,529	-2.8	18,939	2,579	22,899	21,628	-5.6	10,008	11,478
Oklahoma	7,456	7,697	3.2	5,235	2,462	7,694	6,947	-9.7	3,884	2,978
Oregon	5,313	5,376	1.2	3,729	1,443	4,567	5,023	10.0	17	4,745
Pennsylvania	18,175	18,492	1.7	10,758	7,259	17,698	18,805	6.3	3,933	14,702
Rhode Island[g]	850	868	2.1	697	170	960	967	0.7	617	346
South Carolina	7,323	6,802	-7.1	5,205	1,572	7,912	7,309	-7.6	3,160	4,066
South Dakota	2,820	2,918	3.5	1,180	835	2,732	2,812	2.9	399	2,402
Tennessee	14,283	13,922	-2.5	8,577	5,337	14,961	15,955	6.6	4,878	10,997
Texas	73,444	75,378	2.6	50,071	24,331	74,544	82,130	10.2	11,280	66,820
Utah	3,258	3,142	-3.6	1,945	1,197	3,206	3,063	-4.5	1,262	1,786
Vermont[g]	2,044	1,912	-6.5	597	1,315	2,062	1,963	-4.8	306	1,655
Virginia	11,140	11,727	5.3	11,507	220	12,345	11,568	-6.3	1,276	10,168
Washington	16,335	18,232	11.6	7,622	10,605	16,412	18,181	10.8	2,285	15,848
West Virginia	3,404	3,525	3.6	1,724	1,327	3,257	3,293	1.1	1,086	1,744

Continued on the next page

APPENDIX TABLE 1 (continued)
Admissions and releases of sentenced prisoners by Jurisdiction, 2011 and 2012

Jurisdiction	Admissions during—[a]					Releases during—[b]				
	2011 Total	2012 Total	Percent change, 2011–2012	2012 New court commitments[c]	2012 Parole violations[c,d]	2011 Total	2012 Total	Percent change, 2011–2012	2012 Unconditional[c,e]	2012 Conditional[c,f]
Wisconsin	6,411	6,200	-3.3	3,774	2,426	7,825	7,724	-1.3	467	7,213
Wyoming	857	907	5.8	770	137	787	878	11.6	213	659

Note: As of December 31, 2001, sentenced felons from the District of Columbia are the responsibility of the Federal Bureau of Prisons.

/Not reported.

[a]Counts based on prisoners with a sentence of more than 1 year. Counts exclude transfers, escapes, and those absent without leave (AWOL). Totals include other conditional release violators, returns from appeal or bond, and other admissions. See *Methodology*.

[b]Counts based on prisoners with a sentence of more than 1 year. Counts exclude transfers, escapes, and those absent without leave (AWOL). Totals include deaths, releases to appeal or bond, and other releases. See *Methodology*.

[c]Alaska did not report type of admission or release. Total admissions and releases include Alaskan reported values, but state and national totals by type of admission and release do not.

[d]Includes all conditional release violators returned to prison for either violations of conditions of release or for new crimes.

[e]Includes releases to probation, supervised mandatory releases, and other unspecified conditional releases.

[f]Includes expirations of sentence, communtations, and other unconditional releases.

[g]Prisons and jails form one integrated system. Data include total jail and prison populations.

[h]State updated 2011 admission and release totals.

[i]State did not report 2012 NPS data. Total number of admissions and releases imputed, and types of admission and release based on 2011 distribution. See *Methodology*.

[j]Changes made in the legislature to reduce discretionary paroles in 2011 are reflected in a higher parole rate in 2012.

Source: Bureau of Justice Statistics, National Prisoner Statistics Program, 2011–2012.

APPENDIX TABLE 2
Estimated unconditional releases from state prison, by race, Hispanic origin, and most serious offense, 1991, 2001, 2006, and 2011

Most serious offense[c]	1991[a]		2001[b]			2006[b]			2011[b]		
	White	Black	White[d]	Black[d]	Hispanic	White[d]	Black[d]	Hispanic	White[d]	Black[d]	Hispanic
Total	100%	100%	100%	100%	100%	100%	100%	100%	100%	100%	100%
Violent	26.2%	29.5%	26.5%	27.1%	32.9%	22.1%	27.7%	30.5%	20.4%	23.3%	24.6%
Murder[e]	1.4	1.1	0.8	1.0	1.5	0.6	0.8	1.0	0.5	0.7	0.6
Negligent manslaughter	2.3	1.7	0.8	0.6	1.1	0.7	0.5	0.8	0.6	0.5	0.6
Rape/sexual assault	8.8	4.1	9.2	3.9	5.9	6.7	4.5	6.7	5.4	2.9	4.5
Robbery	6.5	13.2	5.4	11.1	10.2	4.0	9.9	8.0	3.5	8.4	5.4
Assault	5.3	8.2	8.1	9.2	11.7	8.1	10.2	11.7	8.0	8.8	10.7
Other violent	2.0	1.2	2.1	1.4	2.6	2.2	1.8	2.4	2.3	2.0	2.8
Property	44.1%	41.9%	41.2%	27.2%	25.4%	36.7%	26.6%	22.8%	38.8%	25.5%	28.0%
Burglary	18.9	16.5	17.1	11.1	12.8	12.9	9.7	10.5	13.9	10.7	10.2
Larceny	10.9	13.1	8.6	7.6	4.3	8.4	7.8	4.7	8.0	6.3	5.7
Motor vehicle theft	2.3	2.3	2.6	1.9	3.0	2.5	1.8	2.5	3.3	1.6	5.4
Fraud	7.3	6.0	7.0	3.8	1.7	8.0	4.7	3.0	6.2	3.8	2.5
Other property	4.8	4.1	6.0	2.8	3.6	5.0	2.6	2.2	7.4	3.1	4.2
Drug	12.1%	20.8%	16.3%	35.9%	31.4%	18.2%	31.4%	27.0%	22.0%	33.1%	31.5%
Possession	4.4	9.4	7.3	11.9	6.2	7.9	11.6	13.0	6.8	6.6	7.2
Other drug[f]	7.7	11.4	9.0	24.0	25.2	10.3	19.8	14.0	15.2	26.5	24.3
Public order[g]	14.3%	5.7%	15.6%	9.4%	9.8%	22.2%	13.9%	19.3%	17.3%	17.0%	15.4%
Other/unspecified[h]	3.2%	2.1%	0.4%	0.3%	0.5%	0.7%	0.4%	0.3%	1.5%	1.1%	0.5%
Number of unconditional releases	24,877	26,248	44,385	47,824	26,084	50,407	54,313	29,623	49,594	53,437	29,146

Note: Based on prisoners with a sentence of more than 1 year released from state prison by expirations of sentence, commutations, and other unconditional releases. Detail may not sum to total due to rounding, missing offense data, and race categories not shown. Release totals from National Prisoner Statistics Program. Offense distribution based on National Corrections Reporting Program administrative data. Estimates may vary from those previously published due to differences in methodology.

[a]Race data are weighted to represent the race/Hispanic origin distribution from the 1991 Survey of Inmates in State Correctional Facilities. The U.S. Office of Management and Budget published guidelines on the collection and reporting of Hispanic origin in 1997 (http://www.whitehouse.gov/omb/fedreg_1997standards/) and few states collected Hispanic origin data in 1991. Persons of Hispanic or Latino origin are included in the white and black categories. See *Methodology*.

[b]Race and Hispanic origin data are weighted to represent the race/ethnicity distribution from the 2004 Survey of Inmates in State Correctional Facilities. See *Methodology*.

[c]Most serious offense refers to the original offense for which an inmate was sentenced, not the incident causing the parole revocation.

[d]Excludes persons of Hispanic or Latino origin and persons of two or more races.

[e]Includes nonnegligent manslaughter.

[f]Includes drug trafficking.

[g]Includes weapons, drunk driving, and court offenses; habitual offender sanctions; commercialized vice, morals, and decency offenses; and liquor law violations and other public order offenses.

[h]Includes juvenile offenses and other unspecified offense categories.

Sources: Bureau of Justice Statistics, National Prisoner Statistics Program and National Corrections Reporting Program, 1991, 2001, 2006, and 2011; and Survey of Inmates in State Correctional Facilities, 1991 and 2004.

APPENDIX TABLE 3
Sentenced state and federal prisoners admitted, by age, sex, race, and Hispanic origin, 2012

Age group	Total[a]	Male					Female				
		All male[a,b]	White[c]	Black[c]	Hispanic	Other[b,c]	All female[a,b]	White[c]	Black[c]	Hispanic	Other[b,c]
Total[d]	100%	100%	100%	100%	100%	100%	100%	100%	100%	100%	100%
18–19	3.5	3.8	2.4	5.1	3.8	3.4	1.5	1.2	2.2	2.1	0.5
20–24	17.7	18.1	15.3	20.0	19.0	18.3	14.5	13.8	15.1	15.0	15.7
25–29	19.3	19.1	18.0	18.3	21.2	21.5	20.6	20.9	17.3	22.5	23.0
30–34	16.7	16.5	16.3	15.4	18.2	16.5	18.8	18.4	17.5	20.3	21.3
35–39	12.4	12.2	12.5	10.8	13.3	14.0	14.0	14.2	13.5	14.6	13.6
40–44	10.9	10.7	12.2	9.9	9.9	10.2	12.2	12.9	12.8	10.9	9.8
45–49	9.0	8.8	10.4	9.0	7.0	7.5	9.9	10.0	11.3	8.7	8.7
50–54	5.8	5.8	7.0	6.2	3.9	4.7	5.3	5.4	6.5	3.8	4.6
55–59	2.6	2.6	3.3	2.8	1.8	1.7	2.0	2.1	2.6	1.4	1.5
60–64	1.1	1.1	1.5	1.1	0.8	0.8	0.7	0.7	0.7	0.4	0.7
65 or older	0.6	0.6	1.0	0.4	0.4	0.6	0.3	0.3	0.3	0.2	0.1
Number of admitted prisoners	609,781	542,940	172,843	198,251	126,005	45,841	66,841	32,685	15,360	10,925	7,872

Note: Counts based on prisoners admitted to serve a sentence of more than 1 year under the jurisdiction of state or federal correctional officials. Excludes transfers, escapes, and those absent without leave (AWOL). Totals for all admissions include other conditional release violators, returns from appeal or bond, and other admissions. Missing data were imputed for Illinois and Nevada. See *Methodology*.

[a]Detail may not sum to total due to rounding, inmates age 17 or younger, and missing race/Hispanic origin data.

[b]Includes American Indians, Alaska Natives, Asians, Native Hawaiians, other Pacific Islanders, and persons identifying two or more races.

[c]Excludes persons of Hispanic or Latino orgin.

[d]Includes persons age 17 or younger.

Sources: Bureau of Justice Statistics, National Prisoner Statistics Program, 2012; Federal Justice Statistics Program, 2011–2012; National Corrections Reporting Program, 2011; and Survey of Inmates in State and Local Correctional Facilities, 2004.

APPENDIX TABLE 4
Sentenced state and federal prisoners, by age, sex, race, and Hispanic origin, December 31, 2012

Age group	Total[a]	Male					Female				
		All male[a,b]	White[c]	Black[c]	Hispanic	Other[b,c]	All female[a,b]	White[c]	Black[c]	Hispanic	Other[b,c]
Total[d]	100%	100%	100%	100%	100%	100%	100%	100%	100%	100%	100%
18–19	1.3%	1.4%	0.8%	1.7%	1.5%	1.3%	0.8%	0.6%	0.9%	1.2%	0.0%
20–24	12.1	12.2	9.4	13.8	13.4	12.5	11.0	9.9	11.5	12.9	12.1
25–29	15.8	15.7	13.8	15.9	17.9	18.2	17.3	17.0	16.2	20.0	20.7
30–34	16.7	16.6	14.9	16.9	18.8	17.9	18.1	17.8	17.5	20.0	20.7
35–39	13.7	13.6	12.5	13.8	15.3	14.9	14.4	14.6	14.1	14.7	13.8
40–44	12.5	12.4	13.3	12.0	12.0	11.6	13.5	14.0	13.7	12.4	12.1
45–49	10.9	10.9	12.5	10.6	9.0	9.2	11.5	11.7	12.4	9.4	9.5
50–54	8.0	8.1	10.0	7.7	5.9	6.8	7.4	7.7	7.7	5.3	6.9
55–59	4.5	4.6	5.9	4.2	3.3	3.6	3.6	3.6	3.8	2.9	3.4
60–64	2.3	2.4	3.4	1.8	1.6	1.9	1.5	1.8	1.3	1.2	0.9
65 or older	1.9	2.0	3.4	1.2	1.2	1.6	1.0	1.2	0.4	0.6	0.9
Number of sentenced prisoners	1,511,480	1,410,191	451,252	527,768	315,234	115,937	101,289	49,352	23,386	16,968	11,584

Note: Counts based on prisoners with a sentence of more than 1 year under the jurisdiction of state or federal correctional officials. Missing data were imputed for Illinois and Nevada. See *Methodology*.

[a]Detail may not sum to total due to rounding, inmates age 17 or younger, and missing race/Hispanic origin data.

[b]Includes American Indians, Alaska Natives, Asians, Native Hawaiians, other Pacific Islanders, and persons identifying two or more races.

[c]Excludes persons of Hispanic or Latino orgin.

[d]Includes persons age 17 or younger.

Sources: Bureau of Justice Statistics, National Prisoner Statistics Program, 2012; Federal Justice Statistics Program, 2012; National Corrections Reporting Program, 2011; and Survey of Inmates in State and Local Correctional Facilities, 2004.

Sentenced state and federal prisoners released, by age, sex, race, and Hispanic origin, 2012

Age group	Total[a]	Male					Female				
		All male[a,b]	White[c]	Black[c]	Hispanic	Other[b,c]	All female[a,b]	White[c]	Black[c]	Hispanic	Other[b,c]
Total[d]	100%	100%	100%	100%	100%	100%	100%	100%	100%	100%	100%
18–19	1.3%	1.2%	0.8%	1.6%	1.3%	1.1%	2.1%	0.4%	0.7%	10.3%	0.5%
20–24	14.0	14.2	12.0	15.1	15.5	14.4	12.6	10.9	10.7	20.6	12.1
25–29	19.0	19.0	17.5	18.5	21.4	20.6	19.1	19.5	16.7	20.2	20.7
30–34	17.6	17.5	16.6	17.0	19.3	18.0	18.2	18.8	17.4	15.7	20.3
35–39	13.3	13.2	12.8	12.3	14.5	14.6	14.5	14.9	14.3	13.6	14.4
40–44	12.0	11.8	13.0	11.4	11.0	11.2	13.1	13.9	14.1	9.6	12.8
45–49	10.3	10.2	11.6	10.5	8.1	9.3	10.7	11.4	13.6	5.7	9.3
50–54	6.9	7.0	8.2	7.4	4.9	6.1	6.0	6.2	8.2	2.2	5.6
55–59	3.2	3.3	3.8	3.7	2.2	2.5	2.2	2.3	2.7	0.8	2.4
60–64	1.4	1.5	1.8	1.5	1.0	1.2	0.9	1.0	1.0	0.4	0.8
65 or older	0.9	1.0	1.5	0.7	0.7	0.8	0.4	0.5	0.4	0.1	0.3
Number of released prisoners	637,411	568,556	181,841	208,415	130,107	48,193	68,855	33,758	15,934	11,038	8,125

Note: Counts based on prisoners admitted to serve a sentence of more than 1 year under the jurisdiction of state or federal correctional officials. Excludes transfers, escapes, and those absent without leave (AWOL). Totals for all admissions include other conditional release violators, returns from appeal or bond, and other admissions. Missing data were imputed for Illinois and Nevada. See *Methodology*.

[a]Detail may not sum to total due to rounding, inmates age 17 or younger, and missing race/Hispanic origin data.

[b]Includes American Indians, Alaska Natives, Asians, Native Hawaiians, other Pacific Islanders, and persons identifying two or more races.

[c]Excludes persons of Hispanic or Latino orgin.

[d]Includes persons age 17 or younger.

Sources: Bureau of Justice Statistics, National Prisoner Statistics Program, 2012; Federal Justice Statistics Program, 2011–2012; National Corrections Reporting Program, 2011; and Survey of Inmates in State and Local Correctional Facilities, 2004.

APPENDIX TABLE 6
Total state and federal prisoners, by sex, December 31, 2011 and 2012

Jurisdiction	2011			2012			Percent change, 2011–2012		
	Total	Males	Females	Total	Males	Females	Total	Males	Females
U.S. Total	1,598,968	1,487,561	111,407	1,570,397	1,461,625	108,772	-1.8%	-1.7%	-2.4%
Federal[a]	216,362	202,462	13,900	217,815	203,766	14,049	0.7%	0.6%	1.1%
State	1,382,606	1,285,099	97,507	1,352,582	1,257,859	94,723	-2.2%	-2.1%	-2.9%
Alabama	32,270	29,696	2,574	32,431	29,782	2,649	0.5	0.3	2.9
Alaska[b]	5,597	4,932	665	5,633	4,934	699	0.6	0.0	5.1
Arizona	40,020	36,470	3,550	40,080	36,447	3,633	0.1	-0.1	2.3
Arkansas	16,108	14,995	1,113	14,654	13,594	1,060	-9.0	-9.3	-4.8
California	149,569	141,382	8,187	134,534	128,436	6,098	-10.1	-9.2	-25.5
Colorado	21,978	19,957	2,021	20,462	18,739	1,723	-6.9	-6.1	-14.7
Connecticut[b]	18,324	17,090	1,234	17,530	16,312	1,218	-4.3	-4.6	-1.3
Delaware[b]	6,739	6,202	537	6,914	6,348	566	2.6	2.4	5.4
Florida	103,055	95,913	7,142	101,930	94,945	6,985	-1.1	-1.0	-2.2
Georgia	55,944	52,027	3,917	55,457	51,868	3,589	-0.9	-0.3	-8.4
Hawaii[b]	6,037	5,304	733	5,831	5,143	688	-3.4	-3.0	-6.1
Idaho	7,739	6,854	885	7,985	6,977	1,008	3.2	1.8	13.9
Illinois[c]	48,427	45,562	2,865	49,348	46,599	2,749	1.9	2.3	-4.0
Indiana	28,906	26,406	2,500	28,831	26,265	2,566	-0.3	-0.5	2.6
Iowa[d]	9,116	8,378	738	8,733	7,949	784	-4.2	-5.1	6.2
Kansas[d]	9,327	8,647	680	9,682	8,952	730	3.8	3.5	7.4
Kentucky	21,545	19,091	2,454	22,110	19,425	2,685	2.6	1.7	9.4
Louisiana	39,710	37,326	2,384	40,172	37,783	2,389	1.2	1.2	0.2
Maine	2,145	1,981	164	2,108	1,944	164	-1.7	-1.9	0.0
Maryland	22,558	21,576	982	21,522	20,646	876	-4.6	-4.3	-10.8
Massachusetts	11,623	10,832	791	11,308	10,549	759	-2.7	-2.6	-4.0
Michigan	42,940	41,031	1,909	43,636	41,647	1,989	1.6	1.5	4.2
Minnesota	9,800	9,156	644	9,938	9,228	710	1.4	0.8	10.2
Mississippi	21,386	19,808	1,578	22,319	20,652	1,667	4.4	4.3	5.6
Missouri	30,833	28,258	2,575	31,247	28,544	2,703	1.3	1.0	5.0
Montana	3,678	3,274	404	3,609	3,210	399	-1.9	-2.0	-1.2
Nebraska	4,616	4,247	369	4,705	4,352	353	1.9	2.5	-4.3
Nevada[c]	12,778	11,811	967	12,883	11,845	1,038	0.8	0.3	7.3
New Hampshire	2,614	2,444	170	2,790	2,583	207	6.7	5.7	21.8
New Jersey	23,834	22,762	1,072	23,225	22,164	1,061	-2.6	-2.6	-1.0
New Mexico	6,998	6,366	632	6,727	6,096	631	-3.9	-4.2	-0.2
New York	55,436	53,124	2,312	54,210	51,963	2,247	-2.2	-2.2	-2.8
North Carolina	39,440	36,800	2,640	37,136	34,675	2,461	-5.8	-5.8	-6.8
North Dakota	1,423	1,276	147	1,512	1,341	171	6.3	5.1	16.3
Ohio	50,964	47,061	3,903	50,876	47,008	3,868	-0.2	-0.1	-0.9
Oklahoma	25,977	23,558	2,419	25,225	22,728	2,497	-2.9	-3.5	3.2
Oregon	14,510	13,387	1,123	14,840	13,609	1,231	2.3	1.7	9.6
Pennsylvania	51,578	48,795	2,783	51,125	48,380	2,745	-0.9	-0.9	-1.4
Rhode Island[b]	3,337	3,158	179	3,318	3,128	190	-0.6	-0.9	6.1
South Carolina	22,914	21,528	1,386	22,388	21,051	1,337	-2.3	-2.2	-3.5
South Dakota	3,535	3,094	441	3,650	3,227	423	3.3	4.3	-4.1
Tennessee	28,479	26,070	2,409	28,411	26,048	2,363	-0.2	-0.1	-1.9
Texas	172,224	158,036	14,188	166,372	152,823	13,549	-3.4	-3.3	-4.5
Utah	6,879	6,266	613	6,962	6,323	639	1.2	0.9	4.2
Vermont[b]	2,053	1,905	148	2,034	1,907	127	-0.9	0.1	-14.2
Virginia	38,130	35,321	2,809	37,044	34,150	2,894	-2.8	-3.3	3.0
Washington	17,847	16,452	1,395	17,271	15,934	1,337	-3.2	-3.1	-4.2
West Virginia	6,826	6,074	752	7,070	6,265	805	3.6	3.1	7.0
Wisconsin	22,657	21,472	1,185	22,600	21,375	1,225	-0.3	-0.5	3.4
Wyoming	2,183	1,944	239	2,204	1,966	238	1.0	1.1	-0.4

Note: Jurisdiction refers to the legal authority of state or federal correctional officials over a prisoner, regardless of where the prisoner is held. Counts are based on prisoners of any sentence length under the jurisdiction of state or federal correctional officials. As of December 31, 2001, sentenced felons from the District of Columbia are the responsibility of the Federal Bureau of Prisons.

[a]Includes inmates held in nonsecure privately operated community corrections facilities and juveniles held in contract facilities.

[b]Prisons and jails form one integrated system. Data include total jail and prison populations.

[c]State did not submit 2012 National Prisoner Statistics (NPS) Program data, so population estimates for 2012 are imputed. See *Methodology* for discussion of imputation strategy.

[d]Change in reporting methods. See *National Prisoner Statistics Program jurisdiction notes*.

Source: Bureau of Justice Statistics, National Prisoner Statistics Program, 2011–2012.

APPENDIX TABLE 7
Prisoners held in the custody of private prisons and local jails, December 31, 2011 and 2012

Jurisdiction	Inmates held in private prisons[a]				Inmates held in local jails			
	2011	2012	Percent change 2011–2012	Percentage of total jurisdiction, 2012	2011	2012	Percent change 2011–2012	Percentage of total jurisdiction, 2012
U.S. Total	130,972	137,220	4.8%	8.7%	82,053	83,603	1.9%	5.3%
Federal[b]	38,546	40,446	4.9	18.6	1,439	795	-44.8	0.4
State	92,426	96,774	4.7%	7.1%	80,614	82,808	2.7%	6.1%
Alabama	545	538	-1.3	1.7	2,148	2,382	10.9	7.3
Alaska[c]	1,688	1,733	2.7	30.8	0	0	0.0	0.0
Arizona	6,457	6,435	-0.3	16.1	0	0	0.0	0.0
Arkansas	0	0	0.0	0.0	883	584	-33.9	4.0
California	697	608	-12.8	0.5	57	0	-100.0	0.0
Colorado	4,303	3,939	-8.5	19.3	116	134	15.5	0.7
Connecticut[c]	855	817	-4.4	4.7	0	0	0.0	0.0
Delaware[c]	0	0	0.0	0.0	0	0	0.0	0.0
Florida	11,827	11,701	-1.1	11.5	1,267	1,197	-5.5	1.2
Georgia	5,615	7,900	40.7	14.2	3,100	4,896	57.9	8.8
Hawaii[c]	1,767	1,636	-7.4	28.1	0	0	0.0	0.0
Idaho	2,332	2,725	16.9	34.1	588	467	-20.6	5.8
Illinois[d]	0	/	/	/	0	/	/	/
Indiana	2,952	4,251	44.0	14.7	1,504	797	-47.0	2.8
Iowa	0	0	0.0	0.0	0	0	0.0	0.0
Kansas	74	83	12.2	0.9	1	0	-100.0	0.0
Kentucky	2,050	812	-60.4	3.7	7,190	8,487	18.0	38.4
Louisiana	2,951	2,956	0.2	7.4	20,866	21,571	3.4	53.7
Maine	0	0	0.0	0.0	110	72	-34.5	3.4
Maryland	78	27	-65.4	0.1	151	178	17.9	0.8
Massachusetts	0	0	0.0	0.0	163	196	20.2	1.7
Michigan	0	0	0.0	0.0	36	42	16.7	0.1
Minnesota	0	0	0.0	0.0	562	614	9.3	6.2
Mississippi	4,669	4,334	-7.2	19.4	5,996	6,528	8.9	29.2
Missouri	0	0	0.0	0.0	0	0	0.0	0.0
Montana	1,418	1,418	0.0	39.3	523	488	-6.7	13.5
Nebraska	0	0	0.0	0.0	56	32	-42.9	0.7
Nevada[d]	0	/	/	/	100	102	2.0	0.8
New Hampshire	0	0	0.0	0.0	20	43	115.0	1.5
New Jersey	2,887	2,717	-5.9	11.7	200	109	-45.5	0.5
New Mexico	2,853	2,999	5.1	44.6	0	0	0.0	0.0
New York	0	0	0.0	0.0	14	0	-100.0	0.0
North Carolina	30	30	0.0	0.1	0	0	0.0	0.0
North Dakota	0	0	0.0	0.0	55	106	92.7	7.0
Ohio	3,004	5,343	77.9	10.5	0	0	0.0	0.0
Oklahoma	6,026	6,423	6.6	25.5	2,088	2,373	13.6	9.4
Oregon	0	0	0.0	0.0	0	0	0.0	0.0
Pennsylvania	1,195	1,219	2.0	2.4	609	489	-19.7	1.0
Rhode Island[c]	0	0	0.0	0.0	0	0	0.0	0.0
South Carolina	20	16	-20.0	0.1	366	374	2.2	1.7
South Dakota	11	15	36.4	0.4	73	64	-12.3	1.8
Tennessee	5,147	5,165	0.3	18.2	8,660	8,618	-0.5	30.3
Texas	18,603	18,617	0.1	11.2	11,906	10,814	-9.2	6.5
Utah	0	0	0.0	0.0	1,529	1,574	2.9	22.6
Vermont[c]	522	504	-3.4	24.8	0	0	0.0	0.0
Virginia	1,569	1,559	-0.6	4.2	7,474	7,389	-1.1	19.9
Washington	0	0	0.0	0.0	386	279	-27.7	1.6
West Virginia	0	0	0.0	0.0	1,677	1,735	3.5	24.5
Wisconsin	36	18	-50.0	0.1	149	70	-53.0	0.3
Wyoming	245	236	-3.7	10.7	9	4	-55.6	0.2

Note: As of December 31, 2001, sentenced felons from the District of Columbia are the responsibility of the Federal Bureau of Prisons.
/Not reported.
[a]Includes prisoners held in the jurisdiction's own private facilities, as well as private facilities in another state.
[b]Includes federal prisoners held in nonsecure, privately operated facilities (8,932), as well as prisoners on home confinement (2,659).
[c]Prisons and jails form one integrated system. Data include total jail and prison populations.
[d]State did not submit 2012 National Prisoner Statistics (NPS) Program data. Local jail value for Nevada estimated based on 2011 data.
Source: Bureau of Justice Statistics, National Prisoner Statistics Program, 2011, 2012.

APPENDIX TABLE 8
Reported state and federal noncitizen inmates and inmates under age 18, December 31, 2012

Jurisdiction	Noncitizen inmates			Inmates under age 18		
	Total	Male	Female	Total	Male	Female
U.S. total	92,892	89,030	3,862	1,325	1,276	49
Federal*	28,959	26,923	2,036	0	0	0
State	63,933	62,107	1,826	1,325	1,276	49
Alabama	199	197	2	88	87	1
Alaska[a,b]	0	0	0	0	0	0
Arizona	4,892	4,769	123	69	61	8
Arkansas	183	175	8	17	15	2
California[c]	15,079	14,745	334	0	0	0
Colorado[d]	1,655	1,592	63	7	7	0
Connecticut[a]	595	572	23	106	102	4
Delaware[a]	304	287	17	12	12	0
Florida[e]	9,976	9,631	345	196	185	11
Georgia	2,720	2,596	124	93	92	1
Hawaii[a]	287	269	18	0	0	0
Idaho	0	0	0	0	0	0
Illinois[f]	/	/	/	/	/	/
Indiana	565	556	9	27	26	1
Iowa	263	257	6	8	8	0
Kansas	336	332	4	4	4	0
Kentucky	247	229	18	0	0	0
Louisiana	125	121	4	38	38	0
Maine	23	22	1	1	1	0
Maryland[d]	651	634	17	24	23	1
Massachusetts[b]	1,025	972	53	1	1	0
Michigan	617	595	22	91	89	2
Minnesota	555	545	10	7	7	0
Mississippi	14	14	0	8	8	0
Missouri[d]	533	499	34	8	8	0
Montana	17	16	1	0	0	0
Nebraska	239	238	1	9	9	0
Nevada[f]	/	/	/	/	/	/
New Hampshire	118	110	8	0	0	0
New Jersey	1,466	1,435	31	7	6	1
New Mexico	174	170	4	0	0	0
New York[d]	4,321	4,196	125	136	132	4
North Carolina	1,569	1,534	35	119	115	4
North Dakota	12	11	1	0	0	0
Ohio	563	545	18	30	30	0
Oklahoma[d]	0	0	0	16	14	2
Oregon	1,233	1,212	21	0	0	0
Pennsylvania	1,071	1,043	28	22	21	1
Rhode Island[a]	69	68	1	0	0	0
South Carolina	493	473	20	32	31	1
South Dakota	76	75	1	0	0	0
Tennessee[d]	276	262	14	19	19	0
Texas	8,808	8,592	216	86	81	5
Utah	351	343	8	2	2	0
Vermont[a]	26	25	1	2	2	0
Virginia	619	603	16	3	3	0
Washington	916	890	26	24	24	0
West Virginia	18	17	1	0	0	0
Wisconsin	613	601	12	13	13	0
Wyoming	41	39	2	0	0	0

Note: The definition of non-U.S. citizen varies across jurisdictions. Use caution when interpreting these statistics.

*The Federal Bureau of Prisons does not house inmates age 17 or younger in federal facilities; 105 such inmates were housed in contract facilities in 2012.

[a]Prisons and jails form one integrated system. Data include total jail and prison populations.

[b]Number of U.S. citizens based only on inmates who reported their citizenship.

[c]Non-U.S. citizens are defined as inmates held by Immigrations and Customs Enforcement (ICE).

[d]Non-U.S. citizens are defined as foreign-born.

[e]Includes both confirmed and suspected alien inmates.

[f]State did not submit 2012 National Prisoner Statistics (NPS) Program data.

Source: Bureau of Justice Statistics, National Prisoner Statistics Program, 2012.

APPENDIX TABLE 9
Prison facility capacity, custody population, and percent capacity, December 31, 2012

Jurisdiction	Type of capacity measure			Custody population	Custody population as a percent of—	
	Rated	Operational	Design		Lowest capacity[a]	Highest capacity[a]
Federal[b]	128,615	...	...	176,658	137.3%	137.3%
Alabama[c]	...	26,339	13,403	26,230	195.7%	99.6%
Alaska	3,058	3,206	...	4,575	149.6	142.7
Arizona	36,681	41,770	36,681	33,578	91.5	80.4
Arkansas	14,407	14,462	13,863	14,043	101.3	97.1
California[c]	...	123,362	84,130	132,935	158.0	107.8
Colorado	...	14,221	13,178	16,389	124.4	115.2
Connecticut	/	/	/	16,347	/	/
Delaware[c]	5,669	5,210	4,161	6,730	161.7	118.7
Florida[d]	...	113,874	...	99,835	87.7	87.7
Georgia[d]	61,184	56,064	...	55,178	98.4	90.2
Hawaii	...	3,327	2,291	3,661	159.8	110.0
Idaho[c,d]	...	7,270	7,442	7,715	106.1	103.7
Illinois[e]	33,804	52,159	33,804	49,348	146.0	94.6
Indiana	...	29,683	...	23,783	80.1	80.1
Iowa	...	...	7,209	8,735	121.2	121.2
Kansas	9,180	9,233	9,164	9,422	102.8	102.0
Kentucky	12,982	13,212	13,807	12,186	93.9	88.3
Louisiana[d]	18,599	18,858	...	18,601	100.0	98.6
Maine	2,339	2,133	2,339	1,977	92.7	84.5
Maryland	...	24,554	...	21,783	88.7	88.7
Massachusetts	...	...	8,029	11,127	138.6	138.6
Michigan[c,f]	45,116	44,284	...	43,594	98.4	96.6
Minnesota	...	9,099	...	9,421	103.5	103.5
Mississippi[d]	...	25,611	...	15,791	61.7	61.7
Missouri[c]	...	31,386	...	31,205	99.4	99.4
Montana	3,378	...	...	1,677	49.6	49.6
Nebraska[c]	...	3,969	3,175	4,721	148.7	118.9
Nevada[g]	...	11,432	...	12,594	110.2	110.2
New Hampshire[c]	...	2,568	2,190	2,568	117.3	100.0
New Jersey	20,256	21,119	22,728	20,333	100.4	89.5
New Mexico	6,192	7,111	7,111	3,641	58.8	51.2
New York	53,164	54,066	52,587	54,058	102.8	100.0
North Carolina	...	36,670	31,304	37,378	119.4	101.9
North Dakota[c]	1,044	991	1,044	1,413	142.6	135.3
Ohio	38,450	...	...	45,529	118.4	118.4
Oklahoma[c]	18,130	...	...	17,947	99.0	99.0
Oregon	...	...	14,362	14,123	98.3	98.3
Pennsylvania[c]	48,579	48,579	48,579	49,009	100.9	100.9
Rhode Island	3,989	3,774	3,973	3,042	76.6	76.3
South Carolina	...	24,031	...	21,867	91.0	91.0
South Dakota[c]	...	3,676	...	3,582	97.4	97.4
Tennessee	20,762	20,241	...	14,652	72.4	70.6
Texas[c]	166,298	159,816	166,298	136,578	85.5	82.1
Utah	...	7,030	7,270	5,309	75.5	73.0
Vermont	1,681	1,681	1,322	1,530	115.7	91.0
Virginia[c]	30,712	...	...	28,149	91.7	91.7
Washington	16,421	15,948	...	16,919	106.1	103.0
West Virginia	4,560	5,390	4,560	5,335	117.0	99.0
Wisconsin[c]	...	...	17,136	22,401	130.7	130.7
Wyoming	2,288	2,288	2,407	1,951	85.3	81.1

...Not available. Specific type of capacity is not measured by state.

/ Not reported. State does not report any capacity data.

[a]Population counts are based on the number of inmates held in custody in facilities operated by the jurisdiction. Excludes inmates held in local jails, other states, or private facilities unless otherwise stated.

[b]Federal custody count reported for the calculation of capacity includes an additional 189 inmates compared to the yearend custody reported in NPS.

[c]State defines capacity in a way that differs from BJS's definition. See individual *National Prisoner Statistics Program jurisdiction notes*.

[d]Private facilities included in capacity and custody counts.

[e]Illinois did not report 2012 National Prisoner Statistics Program data. Capacity counts obtained from DOC website (http://www2.illinois.gov/idoc/reportsandstatistics/Documents/IDOC_Quarterly%20Report_Apr_%202013.pdf), and reflect state prison capacity as of February 28, 2013.

[f]Capacity counts include institution and camp net operating capacities and the population of community programs on December 31 since these programs do not have a fixed capacity.

[g]Nevada did not report 2012 National Prisoner Statistics Program data. Capacity counts obtained from DOC website (http://www.doc.nv.gov/sites/doc/files/pdf/stats/2012/12/SS_QRII_FY13.pdf).

Source: Bureau of Justice Statistics, National Prisoner Statistics Program, 2012.

APPENDIX TABLE 10
Sentenced federal prisoners, by sex and most serious offense, December 31, 2002, 2011, and 2012

Most serious offense	2002			2011			2012			Percent change 2011–2012		
	All inmates	Male	Female	All inmates	Male	Female	All inmates	Male	Female	All inmates	Male	Female
Total	143,040	133,732	9,308	197,050	184,901	12,149	196,574	184,258	12,316	-0.2%	-0.3%	1.4%
Violent	13,586	13,147	438	14,882	14,281	601	11,688	11,226	463	-21.5%	-21.4%	-22.9%
Homicide[a]	1,253	1,191	61	2,839	2,656	183	1,378	1,272	106	-51.5	-52.1	-42.3
Robbery	9,611	9,307	304	8,091	7,844	246	7,110	6,904	206	-12.1	-12.0	-16.4
Other violent	2,722	2,649	73	3,952	3,781	171	3,201	3,050	151	-19.0	-19.3	-11.6
Property	10,033	8,533	1,500	10,697	8,701	1,996	11,568	9,250	2,318	8.1%	6.3%	16.1%
Burglary	230	219	11	410	391	19	172	159	13	-58.0	-59.2	-32.4
Fraud	6,517	5,472	1,045	7,768	6,165	1,603	8,827	6,964	1,863	13.6	13.0	16.2
Other property	3,286	2,842	444	2,519	2,145	374	2,569	2,127	442	2.0	-0.8	18.2
Drug[b]	80,986	74,823	6,163	94,636	87,709	6,927	99,426	92,291	7,135	5.1%	5.2%	3.0%
Public order	37,353	36,219	1,134	68,910	66,805	2,105	72,519	70,219	2,300	5.2%	5.1%	9.3%
Immigration	15,628	15,314	314	22,043	21,427	616	23,700	23,020	680	7.5	7.4	10.3
Weapons	13,781	13,574	207	29,790	29,285	505	30,046	29,567	480	0.9	1.0	-5.1
Other	7,944	7,332	612	17,077	16,094	983	18,773	17,633	1,141	9.9	9.6	16.0
Other/unspecified[c]	1,083	1,009	73	:	:	:	1,372	1,272	100	:%	:%	:%

Note: Counts are based on prisoners with a sentence of more than 1 year under federal jurisdiction. See *Methodology*.
: Not calculated. 2011 data included individuals commiting drug and public order crimes that could not be separated from valid unspecified records.
[a]Includes murder, negligent, and nonnegligent manslaughter.
[b]Includes trafficking, possession, and other drug offenses.
[c]Includes offenses not classified.
Sources: Bureau of Justice Statistics, National Prisoner Statistics Program and Federal Justice Statistics Program, 2002, 2011, and 2012.

APPENDIX TABLE 11
Sentenced federal prisoners, by sex and most serious offense, December 31, 2002, 2011, and 2012

Most serious offense	2002			2011			2012		
	All inmates	Male	Female	All inmates	Male	Female	All inmates	Male	Female
Total	143,040	133,732	9,308	197,050	184,901	12,149	196,574	184,258	12,316
Violent	9.5%	9.8%	4.7%	7.6%	7.7%	4.9%	5.9%	6.1%	3.8%
Homicide[a]	0.9	0.9	0.7	1.4	1.4	1.5	0.7	0.7	0.9
Robbery	6.7	7.0	3.3	4.1	4.2	2.0	3.6	3.7	1.7
Other violent	1.9	2.0	0.8	2.0	2.0	1.4	1.6	1.7	1.2
Property	7.1%	6.4%	16.1%	5.4%	4.7%	16.4%	5.9%	5.0%	18.8%
Burglary	0.2	0.2	0.1	0.2	0.2	0.2	0.1	0.1	0.1
Fraud	4.6	4.1	11.2	3.9	3.3	13.2	4.5	3.8	15.1
Other property	2.3	2.1	4.8	1.3	1.2	3.1	1.3	1.2	3.6
Drug[b]	56.7%	55.9%	66.2%	48.0%	47.4%	57.0%	50.6%	50.1%	57.9%
Public order	26.0%	27.1%	12.2%	35.0%	36.1%	17.3%	36.9%	38.1%	18.7%
Immigration	10.9	11.5	3.4	11.2	11.6	5.1	12.1	12.5	5.5
Weapons	9.6	10.1	2.2	15.1	15.8	4.2	15.3	16.0	3.9
Other	5.6	5.5	6.6	8.7	8.7	8.1	9.6	9.6	9.3
Other/unspecified[c]	0.8%	0.8%	0.8%	:%	:%	:%	0.7%	0.7%	0.8%

Note: Counts are based on prisoners with a sentence of more than 1 year under federal jurisdiction. See *Methodology*.
: Not calculated. 2011 data included individuals commiting drug and public order crimes that could not be separated from valid unspecified records.
[a]Includes murder, negligent, and non-negligent manslaughter.
[b]Includes trafficking, possession, and other drug offenses.
[c]Includes offenses not classified.
Sources: Bureau of Justice Statistics, National Prisoner Statistics Program and Federal Justice Statistics Program, 2002, 2011, and 2012.

www.ingramcontent.com/pod-product-compliance
Lightning Source LLC
Chambersburg PA
CBHW080630290526
45790CB00007B/3002